YOUR
PELVIC
FLOOR
SUCKS

YOUR PELVIC FLOOR SUCKS

But It Doesn't Have To:
A Whole Body Guide to a Better Pelvic Floor

LINDSAY S. MUMMA, DC

For more information, email yourpelvicfloorsucks@pm.me.
ISBN:(paperback) 979-8-88759-493-4
ISBN: (ebook) 979-8-88759-494-1
Library of Congress Control Number: 2023904623

TABLE OF CONTENTS

INTRO

Your pelvic floor actually does suck; that's not just a catchy title. You can squeeze and lift it in the upward sucking motion that most people recognize as a kegel exercise. So yes, your pelvic floor sucks, but it does a lot more, too. And if you're a female, you've been told to kegel 'til the cows come home, but the cows are home and your pelvic floor still isn't working like you want. In that way, perhaps you agree with the statement that your pelvic floor sucks.

Because you picked up this book, I will assume that you either have a pelvic floor that doesn't work effectively at all times (even if your doctor has to ask you multiple times in different ways before you actually admit that), or you're one of those doctors who is recognizing that the advice that WE were given and have been giving to patients is unhelpful at best and harmful at worst, or you're a coach who wants to help clients, OR this book has become so wildly success-ful that all of your friends are talking about it and you're interested.

If you fall under a different category, I can't imagine how you got here, but welcome to the party.

I thought about writing a textbook, but in my experience, no one is interested enough in the study of the pelvic floor, only in the application of its function. And since we're all using our pelvic floors every day, I figured I'd write a book for everyone. It also sounds a bit boring to write a textbook, as most of them are dry and not as approachable as I hope this book to be.

Speaking of hopes, my hope is that **if you're a doctor**, you'll learn new things to approach the care of the pelvic floor, including educating your patients and asking more relevant questions; **if you're a coach**, I hope you'll learn how to best support your clients through any need - not just extremity or spinal injuries, but through pelvic floor rehabilitation (or understand where and when to refer if it's out of your scope); **if you're a patient** (or wish you were a patient because no doctors have helped you yet and you're seeking help), I hope you'll learn where and how to find help and make better decisions about your daily activities and exercises that will improve your pelvic floor function; **if you're a reader** of a best-seller, then I hope you learn something new and become more interesting at dinner parties.

I will state explicitly who this book is *not* for. I welcome anyone to read it, but because pelvic floor dysfunction is such an ongoing problem, there are probably lots of things that we are collectively doing that aren't working well. If you do not have an open mind or a growth mindset, then some of the things I present may actually just make you mad. If you have a growth mindset, you'll welcome the challenge to your existing beliefs, investigate further, and try new things. If you have a fixed mindset, meaning that you're pretty stuck in your way of thinking (Carol Dweck's book *Mindset* is a great read), then you'll probably just dismiss me as an idiot rather than consider that there may be merit in these pages.[1]

The other person this book is *not* for is the person who will read the book but not perform any of the exercises. Each chapter ends with exercises. If you're not willing to try them out and implement them, then this book is not for you.

This book is for those of you who are willing to put forth effort beyond reading.

I will address you, dear reader, as if you are a person with a pelvic floor (because you are) with minimal knowledge of this area of your body. If the verbiage of "your" pelvic floor does not apply to you because yours functions *just fine, thankyouverymuch*, then simply replace "your" with "the" and that ought to set the world right again. But I will address "you" throughout the book because your pelvic floor is a fairly personal region.

There is an exception, and that is when I'm talking about birth. While not everyone will have TMJ dysfunction, it doesn't usually hurt to hear those words applied to you. I know that not everyone who wishes to be a mother is one, so I will refer instead to "a" pregnant or postpartum woman rather than "you."

I also tend to use female rather than male examples. PFD is more common in females than in males and my experience is greater with females than with males, so that's my tendency. But if you're a male with PFD, then these topics apply to you as well.

I hope you learn and I hope you laugh, but I won't even make the joke that you'll pee yourself because that is inappropriate. And you will soon find out that I am always appropriate (except for when I'm not, but it's never about peeing yourself).

DISCLAIMER

You'd think I'd make a health disclaimer because this is a health-related book and I'm not your doctor. Well, by stating that, I just did, didn't I? Take everything you come across with a grain of salt.

But my real disclaimer is that by putting my thoughts and practice ideas into concrete form, I am taking a great personal risk. Not in a life-threatening or dramatic way, but there's a *permanence* here that I'm wary of. I am a student of life. I continue to learn with each patient encounter, personal experience, and further study.

My disclaimer is that this book is what my thoughts currently are on approaching the pelvic floor from a functional standpoint. I hope that in twenty years, there are elements in these pages that still ring true. I also hope that there will be massive swaths of information that I wish I would have known or even face-palm-inducing recommendations that are included in this book that I'm no longer giving to my patients.

Put concisely: I reserve the right to change my mind. But for now, I hope this book will help you change your mind about how your pelvic floor sucks right now.

My attorney wants you to know that following the advice in this book does not guarantee any results and that choosing to participate in the exercises described in this book is completely at your own risk and I assume no responsibility for what you do with this information.

THE END

I know: it's very strange of me to start at the end. However, I have so many books on my shelf - both physically and virtually - that remain unfinished, and I imagine the same is true for you as well. So let's just assume that the chances of your actually finishing this book are slim. Somewhere along the way, your life will distract you from this really great book that you're reading and you'll wind up setting it aside "for another time" that will remain in the distant future. You bought the book, though, which must mean you want to learn something. So in that case, here's the end:

If your pelvic floor and diaphragm are working in synchronization (because your breathing, posture, and activities support this relationship), you have awareness of your pelvic floor, and you stop sucking in all the time, your pelvic floor will already be healthier. If you add in scar tissue mobilization, you'll be next-level functional. And if you intentionally move as you were designed to on a regular basis, beginning with relaxation and then activating muscles rather than just squeezing them, you'll be well on your way to living a life that isn't dictated by your pelvic floor but is, in fact, supported by it.

Doesn't that sound great? Now don't you want to read the whole book so you can figure out how to incorporate all of that?

I really had you excited that you could read a paragraph or two instead of reading a whole book, didn't I? What a jerk.

PART 1

THE BASICS

CHAPTER 1

DEMYSTIFYING BASIC ANATOMY

Now we're at the beginning, even though we're past the end. I'm sure there's a lesson here about the infinite or cyclical nature of life or something. I'll save that for a journal prompt and you can, too. For now, we'll dive into your pelvic floor (metaphorically speaking, of course).

Let's start with the basics. I had a patient tell me that every time she ran, she felt a pulling sensation in her right hamstring. I asked some clarifying questions, did a physical exam, told her that it seemed like it must be a referral from somewhere because her hamstring checked out pretty normal, though her right quads were pretty tight.

Turns out, she thought her hamstring was the muscle on the front of her thigh (it's not). She meant that her quads were pulling when she ran, but had misunderstood for years which were her quads (front of the thigh) and which were her hamstrings (back of the thigh, and so named for how they hang hogs after butchering; now you know). With a smidge of treatment, she was back to running without issue.

I share that little story because it's one of many that are similar. Rather than assume you know what I'm talking about regarding your anatomy, I'll introduce you to the quick version of important anatomical structures. I promise to keep it short and simple so that you don't fall asleep with the book in your hands. You need an understanding of your own anatomy before we really dive in, so I'll lay the groundwork. It will likely help you understand all of this better if you use a mirror and investigate your own parts with as much gusto as you might use when exploring a newly discovered island that's never before been charted. Because that's basically what we're dealing with (although it's a terrible image because your pelvic floor is *not* an island).

You've been walking around on this earth for however long you've been here and have likely never fully investigated your nether regions. Unless, of course, you're a dude. In that case, I will include tidbits in here for you to learn about your own anatomy, function, and dysfunction, but I am fairly certain that you've thoroughly explored the land beneath your belt in exquisite detail. I'm proud of you, truly.

In addition to naming the anatomy, some terminology might be helpful here, so I'm including a few big ones. A *concentric* contraction of a muscle is a shortening contraction. Think of your classic bicep flex to show the ladies which way to the pool. That's a concentric contraction of the bicep. Lowering your arm back down to your side would lengthen the bicep. Lengthening a muscle against load is called an *eccentric* contraction. An *isometric* contraction does not change the length of a muscle.

Palpate means to feel something with your hands. This is not to be confused with palpitate, which is when your heart beats rapidly and irregularly.

Hand waving is not at all clinical, but is a term that I will use, so I want to be sure that my meaning is clear. Picture someone waving away a gnat. That's the gesture I'm referring to, and it's one that we often do when we view something as a throw-away idea or concept. Someone thanks us for picking up their fallen wallet and we wave away the notion that it was any amount of trouble for us to do so. It's a "no big deal" gesture. A "forget about it" gesture. A "don't worry about that" gesture. And it's one that's often used when people say they dribble a bit of urine with a sneeze. Often the people who are hand waving are not being intentionally mean or dismissive.

Randomized Controlled Trial is a type of study wherein the people involved in the study are randomly assigned to groups in order to reduce bias and help improve the study outcomes to be more accurate. This is considered the gold standard for research and is also referred to as an RCT.

Anatomy

For the ladies, there are three holes in your pelvic floor. The front one that you pee out of is called your urethra. Moving back, the next hole is where the magic happens (and by magic I mean ovulation, cervical fluid, and childbirth) and is called your vagina. If you keep heading toward the back of your body, the last hole is your anus.

For the men, you have two holes in your pelvic floor: one at the end of your penis where urine and semen exit and your anus.

Vocab and identifiable parts in relatively simple terms

Pelvic floor: the area between the pubic bone and coccyx (tail bone) that is kind of like a hammock of muscles with holes in it for urine and bowel excretions as well as sexual and reproductive function (plus a lot more that we'll get into)

Perineum: the external region of your pelvic floor (from behind your pubic bone to your coccyx)

- *Perineal body:* the area between the back of the vagina (or in males, the scrotum) and the anus; depending on whose company you're in, you may be referring to this area as your taint or your gooch. I'm not judging you.

Core: technically the area (including the muscles, ligaments, fascia, soft tissue) between your neck and the bottom of your pelvis; for the purposes of this book, we'll focus on your core as the area between your diaphragm and your pelvic floor

Diaphragm: your primary breathing muscle that sits below the lungs on the inside of the ribcage; it's a dome-shaped muscle

Trigger points: a palpable nodule within a muscle that indicates an area of persistent muscular contraction

Fascia: a network of connective tissue that covers and supports every part of your body internally

Vagina: a muscular canal between the uterus internally and the outside of the body

Vulva: the outer part of female genitalia

Cervix: the donut-shaped base of the uterus, located inside of the uppermost part of the vagina

Labia majora and minora: the big and small lip-looking things outside of the opening of the urethra and vagina; the minora are the smaller lips on the inside and the majora are the larger lips on the outside that have pubic hair on them unless you've removed it or you've not yet reached puberty

Penis, scrotum, testicles: I'm trying not to be sexist, so I'm including this; the penis is the external male genitalia. The scrotum is a sack that contains the testicles and helps regulate their temperature. The testicles are the two oval sex organs in males that produce sperm.

Urethra: the tube urine flows out of the bladder to exit the body

Detrusor: the muscle lining the bladder

Levator ani: the largest muscle group in the pelvic floor comprising the puborectalis, pubococcygeus, and coccygeus muscles

Obturator Internus: a key muscle to discuss because it runs both inside and outside of your pelvis; it runs from the back of your femur to the inside of your pelvic bone. It is third from the top of a deep group of hip-rotation muscles that starts with the piriformis, which you may have heard of, and sits directly below the superior gemellus, which you've likely never heard of.

Psoas major and minor: your main hip flexor muscles; these attach from your lumbar spine (low back) to your femur (thigh bone); if your core isn't stable, you will often overuse your hip flexors because they're a close/overlapping neighbor to the core

Pelvic bone: technically the pelvis is one bone, but it's separated into three parts

- *Ilium:* the top one, where you rest your hands when you put your hands "on your hips"
- *Ischium:* the part of your pelvis that you sit on
  - *Ischial tuberosities:* the bony protuberances underneath your butt/at the top of the back of your thighs - which some people call "butt bones"
- *Pubis:* the front part of your pelvis that's just above your genitals
  - *Pubic symphysis:* the joint at the front of your pelvis that connects the two pubic bones together via a fibrocartilaginous (tough and dense) disc

Sacroiliac joints: the joints between your sacrum (the bottom part of your spine) and your ilium (the top of the pelvis); these are often referred to as SI joints

Coccyx: your tailbone; a tiny, moveable bone at the base of your sacrum that is not intended for weight bearing because it is where your tail would be if you had one (so stop slouching and sitting on your tail)

Iliofemoral joints: your hip joints - where your femur (thigh bone) attaches to your pelvis

Thoracolumbar junction: the upper portion of your lower back or the lower portion of your mid back, depending on how you look at the world; this is where your thoracic spine (the rounded part that your mother always told you to keep upright) and your lumbar spine (low back) meet

Diastasis rectus abdominis: separation of the rectus abdominis (six-pack) muscles due to overstretching of the linea alba; this happens naturally during childbirth, exists at birth, can persist if movement milestones are not adequately met; and can be created with repetitive poor loading strategies in any human of any age

Trapezius: muscles on either side of your neck that are used for shrugging your shoulders and where people rub when they do a well-meaning but horrible "shoulder massage;" these muscles actually go from the back of your head, out to the back of your shoulders, and into your midback, attaching along your spine on both sides; these are often just called "traps"

Intra-abdominal pressure (IAP): the steady state pressure within the abdominal cavity; the level of IAP can vary depending on movement, breath, or life state (such as pregnancy, postpartum, or post-surgical)

This isn't something you'll be quizzed on, and I'll try to remind you of these definitions if it's a word we haven't repeatedly used. I may also use lay terms if it makes more sense because that helps keep things more approachable. I've used the terms "gooch" and "taint" when presenting at conferences before because it tends to give people a better idea of what I'm talking about. It might surprise you how very little your doctor is informed about the pelvic floor and its functions. Using a word like taint can help bridge the gap, though some of my more prudent class reviewers have noted my "crass" language. I'm just here to help.

Another definition I want to share is a theory called the Boat Theory. Boat Theory is something that is discussed among pelvic health professionals, though I don't know where the theory originated. The closest thing to a source I could find were pictures from the Continence Foundation of Australia. The idea is to consider a boat that is in the water and tethered to a dock on both sides. The boat represents your pelvic organs - uterus, bladder, rectum - and the ropes holding the boat represent your pelvic ligaments. The water level represents your pelvic floor muscles.

The idea is that if the water level is high enough, the water supports the boat. If the water is too low, then the ropes docking it are overstressed. The theory demonstrates how laxity (stretched, weak muscles) in the pelvic floor can cause further damage to pelvic ligaments and lead to pro-lapse of the pelvic organs. We'll address prolapse later, but I wanted you to have the idea of that image in your head before moving on.

Exercise - Mirror Exploration

Within each chapter, I'll include exercises or activities for you to do. These take the book from theory to application and are crucial to your benefitting from reading this book.

To further the images in your head, it's time to grab a mirror. Lock the door, drop your drawers, and take a peek at your own anatomy. Again, gentlemen: have a field day. Ladies, this might be new for you, but go ahead and get acquainted. With a clean hand, palpate (that just means to feel with your hands) the inside of your vagina and try to find your cervix. This will feel like a fairly hard bump with a hole in the center like a donut that has the same firmness as the end of your nose when you're not fertile and like the lobe of your ear if you're fertile.

We won't get too far into fertility information here, but grab yourself a copy of Toni Weschler's *Taking Charge of Your Fertility* if you're interested.

Identify your labia majora and minora; note your urethra. If you've given birth and know that you've had a perineal tear or episiotomy, check for scar tissue. Like any other scar, this will have a slightly different color and feel than the rest of the surrounding tissues, and the sensation of the area itself may feel different internally.

We'll get more into scar tissue later on, but take note if palpating your scars gives you - clinical term here - the heebie jeebies. Lots of people do not like the feeling of scar tissue. When they touch it, it just doesn't feel *right*, though there's not often an exact explanation for it. Sometimes it feels less (hypoesthesia), sometimes it feels more (hyperesthesia), and sometimes it feels weird or tingly (parasthesia).

We've got the basics covered and ideally you're a bit more familiar with yourself. That wasn't so bad, right? This is just so we have a baseline. You may revisit this exercise at any point because the region is yours to explore.

A note on the exercises from each chapter: do them. The exercises are intentionally laid out as I would prescribe them to patients in my practice so that they unfold in such a way that they create a foundation and then build from there.

CHAPTER 2

BREATHING

I know you thought you were reading a book about the pelvic floor. You still are. But we can't talk about the pelvic floor as if it's an island. What a strange island that would be. Are you picturing it? I am. But like I said before when I encouraged you to investigate this new area with gusto: your pelvic floor is *not* an island. Your pelvic floor is part of a system. We can't talk about the pelvic floor without talking about the diaphragm.

The first thing I want to point out is that the "e" sound in breath is short, meaning it's pronounced like "pet." The "e" sound in breathe is pronounced like "peeve." These are often pronounced correctly, but misspelled frequently, which is clearly one of my pet peeves. The extra e at the end changes things. Now you know, and we can crack on.

Most of you reading this book are probably like most of my patients: you will undervalue and underestimate the importance of breath and this entire section of the book. You will likely tire of how diligently I explain the simple exercise at the end of this chapter (simple does not equate to easy).

You will want to skip past this chapter and the exercise at the end. *Do not.* If you have studied breath or breathing techniques at all, this tendency will be even higher. Another hand waving situation of "I already know that stuff." But I urge you to read this and be a forever student. I am not a master and am still learning myself, but I wish to extend the experiences I've had to help you, and I am truly requesting that you actually read each part of this section and the exercise at the end of the chapter and perform it as described.

If we compare the diaphragm and the pelvic floor anatomy, they are quite similar in appearance. I get that just because things look alike doesn't mean that they function alike. I looked like Brooke Shields when I was younger. I heard it all the time. But I never made money for acting. I did, however, have quite a flair for the dramatics, so maybe I missed out on that. Either way, my point is that similar appearance does not mean similar action.

Sometimes it does. In the case of the diaphragm and pelvic floor, they actually *do* function similarly.

The three holes in a female pelvic floor basically mirror the three holes in the diaphragm. The diaphragm's three holes are the caval opening, esophageal hiatus, and aortic hiatus. These openings are the passageways for structures to pass through the diaphragm.

The diaphragm has three main functions: as a sphincter (to prevent your stomach from rising above your diaphragm as it does in the case of a hiatal hernia), in respiration (breathing), and in stabilization/posture (holding you upright and also creating stability). The pelvic floor's main functions are as a sphincter, in respiration, and in stabilization/posture.[1] The pelvic floor also has additional functions related to sexual function and fertility, but you can see the similar functions of these two structures, which is why the pelvic floor is sometimes also referred to as the pelvic diaphragm.

During respiration, the diaphragm descends as the lungs fill with air on inhale, and the pelvic floor descends as the pressure within the abdominal cavity increases. On exhale, the diaphragm ascends back up into the ribcage and the pelvic floor also rises. Because it is crucial to understand, I will review this point again. As the diaphragm descends (on the inhale), the pelvic floor descends. As the diaphragm rises (on the exhale), your pelvic floor rises. They work together in a synchronous way and improving the function of one improves the function of the other. A 2021 RCT (randomized controlled trial) showed that training the pelvic floor improved the function of the diaphragm.[2]

There's generally some more hand-waving about this, as if breathing is a thing we're all doing automatically and therefore doesn't require our rapt attention. I disagree (obviously, since I'm spending so many words on the topic). The breath is the crucial missing piece for pelvic floor rehabilitation.

But.

The tendency in a lot of pelvic rehab circles (yes, those are things - there's a whole world of people focused on pelvic rehabilitation) is to focus on the exhale. We'll get to that in

Part 3 of this book, so stick around to find out why that's *not* my focus and why I steer people away from that.

The problem is that most people are not allowing their diaphragm to descend during breath and therefore are missing out on the synchronizing activity of the pelvic floor. This then impacts the postural function of the diaphragm as well. The connection between the diaphragm and the pelvic floor via intra-abdominal pressure (the pressure in the abdomen that increases as the diaphragm lowers - which happens with each inhale but can also happen under conscious control) cannot happen adequately if the diaphragm isn't lowering.

If you're sucking your belly in, your pelvic floor will not move in sync with your diaphragm because you've essentially inhibited your diaphragm's motion by preventing its descent with your rectus abdominis (six-pack) muscles. This is true even if you don't have a visible six-pack. Holding tension in your abdomen changes how your diaphragm functions and prevents you from fully utilizing it.

Some people do this intentionally as they've been taught that holding their abs tight will help strengthen their back or keep them more stable.

Most people do this *un*intentionally because of habitually sucking in for aesthetic purposes. It doesn't work, of course. Whenever someone is sucking in, they just look like they're sucking in (and generally uncomfortable) rather than like they're thinner. We all know it, but many of us still insist on sucking in.

A mentor of mine, Dr. Brett Winchester, said years ago that he introduced his patients to the following acceptable circumstances for sucking in:

1. You're getting your picture taken.
2. You're in cocktail attire.
3. You're in a bathing suit.

If any of those three situations ring true, you can suck in. Otherwise, stop holding tension in your abdomen.

A patient of mine asked me if she could suck in if she ran into a particular ex-boyfriend. I thought that was reasonable, given their history, so now my patients hear the four circumstances when it can be considered appropriate to suck in. I'll let you decide if your situation warrants the fourth or not.

Except I'm personally such a zealot that I don't suck in at all,* even for pictures.

Sometimes there's a specific overlap of sucking in and slouching that's really hard to combat. We're going to talk about posture in the next chapter, but for now, know that these habits run deep. If you have tension in your abdomen (either because you're actively (if inadvertently) sucking in or because you've limited your diaphragm's range of motion by slouching), you will not be able to breathe efficiently. You'll still breathe, because if you didn't, you wouldn't be reading this book. But the *efficiency* part would be missing.

---

* I feel obliged to tell you that I did suck in my stomach in 2015. I was in a pageant. Yes, I was Mrs. Raleigh. Technically, I should've been Dr. Raleigh, but that didn't really work for the Mrs. North Carolina people. Anyway, I was wearing a bikini and heels on a stage and the circumstances called for sucking in for posing. Now you know.

Part of our movement's efficiency requirement is to have appropriate co-contraction of the muscles surrounding a region. Each muscle plays a role, and often we discuss muscle actions by describing when they are synergistic (helping), and when they are antagonistic (opposing) other muscles. Your rectus abdominis (six-pack muscles) are antagonistic to your diaphragm. They're not teasing it or truly antagonizing it: they prevent it from fully exerting. Just like your biceps and triceps (front and back of your upper arm muscles) are antagonistic to each other: when one is fully contracted, the other can't be. They limit each other's movements. So if you hold tension in your abdomen with your rectus abdominis muscles (which are designed to flex your spine), you limit your diaphragm's ability to work fully.

If you're pulling your stomach in or you're slouched, your diaphragm still has to get lower in order for your lungs to inflate. If it can't *actually* get lower, then you can raise your chest as an alternative to make it seem like your diaphragm is lower (because if your upper chest rises, your diaphragm technically is lower, relatively speaking). This is the opposite of how your breathing mechanics should work. It becomes even more concerning if we see the abdomen pulling in further as you breathe in.

Your diaphragm lowering has more impact beyond breathing mechanics. When your diaphragm lowers, it actually causes the rest of your organs to move (though your organs move during breath-holding as well).[3] This organ motility (movement) helps improve circulation and function of your abdominal organs (the uterus, ovaries, bladder, intestines, kidneys, etc.). All of these organs need to move in order to function optimally. When you breathe in, your organs should descend with your diaphragm, and then return to their original resting state upon exhale. When you suck in, your diaphragm can't properly lower and your organs move less as a result. You don't have to force them to move if you simply stop preventing them from moving. When you relax your abdomen and breathe fully in 360 degrees, you will allow your organs to move freely. They're still being supported by your pelvic floor, but your pelvic floor is getting movement and blood flow along with your organs, which it needs.

It's important to note that clothing can also restrict your abdominal expansion during breathing. Shapewear might give you smoother lines in a cocktail dress (when you might already be sucking in per the earlier guidelines), but it can also prevent your diaphragm from fully exerting. The same is true for a belt or tight waistband. Keep that in mind when choosing your attire.

The other part of breathing that cannot be overstated is breathing through your nose: both in and out. James Nestor detailed most of the reasons why in his incredible book *Breath*, but the short version is that mouth breathing is truly detrimental to your health and nasal breathing is supportive of it.[4] If you can't breathe through your nose, keep working at it.

I know that sounds like a rude or uncaring solution, but it gets easier the more you do it. In fact, breathing through your nose is like my speaking French. I hardly ever do it, so it seems like I can't. But I did take three years of it in high school, so there's some part of me that sort of remembers. If you were to drop me into a French neighborhood and I just kept speaking French because I was forced to, I'd eventually speak more French. So try it (nasal breathing is what that "it" refers to, but go ahead and speak French, too).

But why am I breathing wrong?

People ask me this question all of the time. How is it that I'm *breathing* wrong? They'll say it with the emphasis as if they simply can't do anything right if they're not even accomplishing this simple task appropriately. We've already gone over all of the complexities of breathing, so I hope you can see that it's pretty easy to mess up.

But I think the majority of dysfunction stems from three things. I have no concrete or direct evidence for this, but from a common sense standpoint, these three reasons seem to cover most scenarios for why people are breathing inappropriately.

1. We sit entirely too much, causing us to slouch (we'll talk about that in the next chapter), which leads us to be unable to breathe with our full core because we lose real estate for our diaphragm to expand downward when we are slouching. Our world is now designed for sitting and it is trained early in life. We typically start sitting kids at five, but I'm seeing this creep up to even younger ages as more and more daycares are

functioning like pre-kindergarten prep schools and involve way more seated activities than free play.

2. We are taught to suck in - both on purpose because someone tells you to suck in your gut or pull your abs in to "stabilize your core" and through mimicry because we see everyone else doing it. Girls are taught to be smaller and boys are taught to have big puffed up chests. Both require sucking in the abdomen, which inhibits the diaphragm. We'll get more into this in the next chapter as well.

3. We're stressed. And even when we're not stressed, we breathe like we're stressed because we're so used to breathing like we're stressed, and that stress-like breathing causes us to neurologically feel stressed. It's a bit of a nasty cycle.

The third point is the one I want to expand on now, since we'll get to the other two in the next chapter. When you're under stress - I'm talking real, physical stress that you are physiologically adapted for: like if a tiger was crouched in the weeds 15 feet away from you - your body responds to that stressor.

Your breathing becomes more shallow and rapid. Your pupils dilate, your heart rate increases, and your digestion slows. You care more about pumping oxygenated blood to your extremities - so you can run or fight - than you do about making sure your last meal gets digested. You probably even breathe through your mouth to take a few gasps of air in.

When you're under stress, your physiology is focused on short-term survival, not long-term thriving.

The good news is: this is actually good for you.[5] You were built to withstand these major stressors in short bursts, and then either escape the stressful situation or die trying. That's a little morbid, but it's accurate. You weren't built to be constantly stressed all of the time. If you're breathing as if you *are* constantly stressed and you're stuck in the cycle of shallow breathing = stress = shallow breathing, your body holds tension in such a way that you're ready to pounce at a moment's notice.

If you're under perceived stress, but instead of a tiger, it's your spouse or your job or your mother-in-law (not mine, she's great), then your body tries to adapt to this chronic state of stress. It can't. We entered into sedentary, largely safe ways of living faster than our physiology could keep up. (Another great book to read would be *Civilized to Death* by Christopher Ryan.)[6] So you take shallow mouth breaths without realizing that your work deadline or traffic or fill-in-the-blank with whatever irks you is causing you to respond as if you're under truly stressful circumstances, and then your physiology responds.

I say "perceived stress" because this is a head nod toward the Polyvagal Theory.[7] It's a beautiful theory by Dr. Stephen Porges that informs a lot of how I live and practice. I do not wish to bastardize the decades of research he's done, but to simplify it as much as possible for brevity, it's a theory that instead of your autonomic nervous system working in a dichotomy (rest/digest or fight/flight), it actually functions in a hierarchy based upon your perception of how safe you are.

The hierarchy consists of three levels: Socialization, Mobilization, and Immobilization. Mobilization is pretty similar to what you learned in high school as the fight/flight part of your nervous system. Immobilization is similar to what you learned as the rest/digest part of your nervous system. Socialization is the component unique to mammals, and gets developed largely in the first year of life for humans.

If you are under a perceived threat, your nervous system will respond differently than if you are under no perceived threat. The hierarchy of your nervous system will typically attempt to work from top down: you'll try to socialize your way out of a problem, then mobilize, then immobilize if those don't work.

You may have heard "fight, flight, or freeze," which is recognizing that sometimes a threat is so great that our nervous system's best bet for helping us to survive is immobilization or freezing. A lot of Dr. Porges' work has helped many trauma victims to recognize that their body didn't betray them by not helping them escape a predatory person or situation, but froze as a result of deep-seeded neurology that helped them to actually survive a situation that fighting or fleeing would likely not have.

My point in addressing this perception of stress is that if you're stressed (or just breathing like you're stressed), you're more likely to hold your body in at least a slightly rigid state, which will cause you to breathe with an increased rate of chest/mouth breathing that further perpetuates the stress response your body is experiencing. Holding tension specifically in your rectus abdominis muscles prevents your diaphragm from lowering to its fullest extent like we talked about because these muscles have an antagonistic relationship. This means the increase in intra-abdominal pressure (IAP) that *should* be reaching your pelvic floor is stopped up around your mid-belly, meaning you're missing the stability of a fully pressurized core, which includes organ motility and blood flow.

An antidote to these three sources of dysfunction is to close your mouth and breathe slowly into your whole core: feel expansion into your entire rib cage, breathe into your back, and prevent upward motion of your shoulders by instead allowing full expansion of your breath into your lower abdomen. Breathe just like the exercise I am about to assign to you at the end of this chapter.

This will allow you to retrain appropriate patterns and disrupt the stress breathing cycle because you wouldn't breathe this way if you were truly under life-threatening stress. The fact that you CAN adopt this slow, measured breathing means that your brain will begin to perceive a much safer environment. In addition to improving your pelvic floor, this will also help improve your stress response in general.

Exercise - Full Core Breathing

Remember that I've already assumed some of you want to skip this part. Don't. We all need repetitions, and it won't hurt to take a few intentional breaths with me here.

I want you to lie flat on the ground. Take your book with you, of course, because otherwise, you won't know what to do next.

Bend your knees, placing your feet flat on the ground, which will help put your diaphragm parallel to your pelvic floor. An easier way to envision that is to recognize that your rib cage is now relatively parallel to your pelvis, which is where it belongs most of the time.

Now inhale (through your nose, of course), and notice where your breath goes. Can you hear your favorite yoga teacher saying that exact line? Many yogis have great awareness of their breath, but still spend a great deal of energy attempting to control it rather than following its most physiological path.

Ideally, when you inhale, your abdomen is relaxed (it should be - you're lying down, for heaven's sake) and expands equally to the front, sides, and back with the increase in intra-abdominal pressure from the diaphragm descending. You will also have a (likely imperceptible) expansion into your pelvic floor.

It's likely that's not the case for you (because this is a huge factor in pelvic floor function and we're assuming yours isn't working well), and rather than your abdomen expanding outward as if into your favorite pair of comfy sweats that you only wear when people who love you - I mean really, truly, unconditionally love you because those pants are embarrassing - are around, your abdomen draws inward and your chest rises toward your head. That's okay, we're only in Chapter 2 and there's hope for you yet. Let's work together to improve your breathing pattern.

If you have some tightness in your belly (go ahead and poke your belly gently and see if it's nice and pliable and jiggly in a way that you hope no one notices), that means you're holding tension in your rectus abdominis muscles (AKA sucking in) and your chest has no choice but to rise toward your head because you have to breathe and your diaphragm has hit a roadblock.

You first must relax your rectus abdominis before you can give your diaphragm its full reign of movement. This is quite tough if you've been a lifelong sucker-inner. But it's necessary and probably the key to this whole book working in your favor.

Place one hand on your chest as if you're going to say The Pledge of Allegiance and one hand on your lower belly. Do not force your belly out intentionally, but attempt to allow it to expand into your lower hand and simultaneously expand forward (toward the ceiling) but not upward (toward your head) into the hand on your chest.

Remember that you're still lying on your back (if you're actually on your back, that was possibly the dumbest thing I could say, but because this part got longer than you were expecting, you may have abandoned the original position I suggested and are now sitting upright, shaking your head at what you think are ridiculous and impossible recommendations, so I wanted to remind you of the directions I'm referencing). If the hand on your chest expands toward the ceiling, that's fine. Your chest, abdomen, and back are all going to expand with breath; I just don't want your chest to rise toward your head. Expanding your chest is fine, but elevating your chest is missing the mark.

I want to ensure that you are not just breathing into the front of your abdomen (think: Buddha belly or beer belly, depending on how spiritual you're feeling). And I also do not want you to push out in order to create expansion. This is not a Buddha belly breath and it's not a forceful expansion.

Now try placing your hands on your sides with your thumbs in the back and fingers wrapped around the lowest part of your rib cage. Depending on how long your torso is, you may be touching the top of your pelvis with your pinky fingers. Breathing into your thumbs will help ensure that you're not just breathing forward (Buddha belly). Breathe in and allow the breath to expand into all ten of your fingers. Notice how upon exhale, the rib cage returns to its original position.

Choose which hand placement you like best and take ten full (but not forceful) breaths.

Ideally you feel a bit more relaxed for having just taken ten full breaths and not so annoyed at how challenging it was to breathe. Like I said, this is paramount. And it actually only gets harder; we're doing this lying down, and it's even harder when you're upright.

Practice this four times per day. I'm not kidding. It will take you approximately two minutes each time you do this. If you cannot commit eight minutes of your day to improving your pelvic floor function, then why did you even buy this book? Improving your breathing will improve your pelvic floor function, and we have to start somewhere.

(In the resources at the end of this book, you'll find all of your exercises in video format.)

CHAPTER 3

POSTURE

I spend a significant amount of time ~~nagging~~ talking to my patients about how they carry themselves. There's not one perfect posture and we're dynamic creatures, so what I want is the posture that best supports all of the body's functions, specifically: breathing. You will not be able to maintain the full diaphragmatic breathing that I explained in the last chapter if your posture does not support this activity. So once we've established how to breathe, we have to establish how to continue breathing in that way when you're doing more than just lying on the ground.

I say all of the time that posture is a choice until it isn't. I won't go too far into the weeds here, but there is a process called creep, hysteresis, and set that Professor Nikolai Bogduk introduced in the 1990s regarding tissue changes.[1] Essentially, your tissues will accommodate your posture and will create the environment that you've asked of them.

I'm going to assume that your posture sucks. I'm glad if it doesn't, but it makes it easier to address dysfunction in a book format if the reader has the dysfunction the author is referencing.

Your posture sucks in the way that you have allowed it to suck. Or even, in some circumstances (like sucking in), encouraged it to suck. My recommendation is to stop allowing it to suck (both in the way that you've perpetuated with poor posture habits and in the way that it will continue to suck unless you do something different and create a change).

Head Positioning

One of the most common ways to have posture that sucks is to hold your head forward (in front of your shoulders). Your head weighs about as much as a bowling ball. And if you had to carry a bowling ball around all day, would you carry it out in front of you, or would you bring it back and rest it as close to your body as possible, so that your skeletal structures could help hold the weight of it?

I use this example all of the time with my patients because nobody would attempt to carry a bowling ball in front of their body if they were stuck with the thing all day. Everyone would bring it back to rest on their shoulder, and that's what I want you to do with your head. As soon as you do this with your head, it will automatically start to change what's happening in the rest of your body. We could spend an entire section of this book talking about the mechanics of your foot, knee, hip, or low back, but if you correct your posture at your head and neck, then it will have downstream effects on the rest of your posture.

We could certainly work with any of your lower extremity biomechanics, but since we're focused on what's happening underneath of your diaphragm, putting your head on top of the rest of your body is a great place to start that.

When you bring your head back on top of your body, your chin is retracting. This may be uncomfortable in a physical sense because you will cause your suboccipital (back of your head/top of your neck) muscles to stretch a bit in a way they're not used to since they had to beef themselves up to carry that beautiful bowling ball around all of these years. It may also be uncomfortable in the sense that you are doing something that causes you to suddenly be aware of an unsightly double-chin. Fear not. With repetition of this movement, you will actually help to strengthen your deep neck flexors (muscles at the front of your neck), so that you won't have to inject botulism into your neck to paralyze it for fear of letting anyone know you've had the privilege of being on this earth longer than your adolescence.

Because you now have your head firmly (if uncomfortably and a little begrudgingly) atop your body, and your mouth is closed because we hammered the nasal breathing thing last chapter, you're legitimately loading your tissues differently than if you weren't doing those things before (which I took the liberty of already assuming about you long ago). But since you're newly self-conscious of your double-chin, here's a quick exercise to help your jaw, your facial physique, your posture, and by proxy, your pelvic floor.

Exercise - TMJ Training

Place one finger under your jaw, behind your chin. It doesn't matter much what finger you choose (though I imagine you have a special one you picked for me for bringing about that double-chin look) or how you position it, as long as it's in the soft part behind your chin and above your neck.

Now, with your mouth closed, press your tongue into the roof of your mouth and feel with your finger what happens under your jaw. The bulging down of those tissues into your fingers is largely created by the exertion of your digastric muscles, which function to open your jaw properly by bringing the mandible (lower jaw) down and back.

Many of my patients with pelvic floor dysfunction (PFD) also experience TMD (what lots of people call "TMJ" but this is a misnomer because temporomandibular joint is not a disorder; it's a joint; temporomandibular disorder is, in fact, a disorder). This is not a coincidence, which is, of course, why I've included this in a book about pelvic floor disorders. I will again assume that you have some amount of TMD, so while we're working on helping your pelvic floor and your double-chin, we'll just knock out that TMD as well.

The next thing I want you to do is to allow your mouth to open while still maintaining contact of your tongue with the roof of your mouth. You do not need to push into the roof of your mouth, but simply place the tip of your tongue behind your upper teeth as if you were about to say "no" and slowly open your mouth and close it again, without jutting your jaw forward. Repeat 10 times. Now we're exercising your digastric muscles, which will help keep your bowling ball in place and will help shape up that double-chin.

Am I hitting the double-chin thing too hard? I honestly don't care how many chins you have, but my goodness, the push-back I get from patients on relaxing their abdomen and bringing their head back on top of their body often starts with the aesthetic changes. I'm just trying to quell those.

Make sure that even though your mouth is open, you're breathing through your nose. You don't need to maintain suction of your tongue on the roof of your mouth, just gently keep the tip of your tongue there.

This is a great exercise to do as a posture break from desk work or at a red light if you've been driving for a while. If you suffer from TMD, it's a good idea to incorporate this exercise at least twice daily.

Joint Centration

The digastric muscles will also help improve the function of your jaw by helping it to move appropriately, which it can now do since your head isn't a day's trip away from your body and is instead resting atop your neck. This actually places a bone in your skull that looks eerily similar to your pelvis, called your sphenoid, atop your pelvis. Having your head over your diaphragm over your pelvic floor will serve you well. While it doesn't feel like it at first, this alignment allows for the most ease within your body because it is now biomechanically as *centrated* as possible.

I actually hesitate to use the word "alignment" because I am a chiropractor. That may surprise you because a lot of chiropractors and their patients seem so focused on the topic. But that's usually because of the idea that bones need to be "realigned" with adjustments. However, the existence of your ligaments, joint capsules, and soft tissues tells me that your bones aren't just flopping out all over the place and requiring a jostling of sorts to get them to fall in line. (With an adjustment, chiropractors introduce motion into joints that are restricted rather than popping bones back into place. I tell my patients all of the time that if their bones were out of place, they'd be down the street at the hospital and not walking into my office.)

Instead of alignment, I tend to focus on joint centration. Joint centration is a concept that is deeply explored in the teachings of Dynamic Neuromuscular Stabilization (DNS), which is the foundation for most of my rehabilitative information and one of the cornerstones of my practice. DNS was founded in Prague by Prof. Pavel Kolar, though their instructors teach all over the world. I have gratefully been learning these concepts since I was in chiropractic college and had Dr. Dave Juehring - a DNS instructor - as a mentor.

Joint centration specifically is in reference to a single joint being in its most centered position, allowing for a balance of stability and mobility. Picture a ball and socket joint (like your shoulder) and assume that when it is centrated, the joint will have its greatest controlled ranges of motion and effectively be in its safest biomechanical positioning for any activity. A centrated joint will also have a minimal amount of muscular activity involved in maintaining the position. In other words, it is an efficient position.

I like to take this concept and apply it broadly to your whole body. I'm referring to your joints being in their most normal, physiological resting positions. For example, whole body centration can't occur if you're standing with more weight on one leg than the other. In that instance, your hips would not be centrated, so therefore your body would be less centrated overall.

But joint centration is merely one concept of the DNS teachings. I have learned so much from every DNS class I've taken, and all of my patient care, classes, and offerings have some elements of DNS baked in. It's what's helped me help others with any amount of core dysfunction (including PFD, of course) more than any other therapy.

Another main focus that most first-time DNS students walk away from a class with is the fundamentals of breathing and how to utilize appropriate breathing and stabilizing strategies to improve performance, treatments, or outcomes in general. It ruins the fallacy of an hourglass figure as ideal and challenges the assumption that holding your stomach tight equates to a stronger core. (And now you can see its influence in my writings.)

Upper Back and Shoulder Positioning

Breath is crucial for maintaining upright posture and vice-versa. If you are slouched forward (caught you, didn't I? Sit up straight, would ya?!), you will have a harder time taking a breath than if you're standing or sitting upright. You'll also have a harder time standing or sitting upright if you're not taking a full core breath. It's a double-edged sword and a self-fulfilling prophecy.

Posture and breath are inextricably linked because the diaphragm, as we've addressed, is also a postural muscle. If you're not lying down, your diaphragm is helping to hold you upright. If you stop relying on it for that function because you perpetually round your shoulders forward, allow your chin to protrude in front of your chest, and slump into your best impression of a 90s emo kid, you'll lose it because your diaphragm won't be exercised and can actually weaken.

Postural Changes in Pregnancy

During pregnancy, there are a lot of postural changes that occur to accommodate an additional person occupying your personal space. These changes - such as your center of gravity shifting forward, your pelvis tilting forward, your lumbar spine extending (arching backward) and your thoracic spine flexing (rounding forward) - are short-lived. Or they ought to be. One of the commonalities I see from my postpartum patients is that they retain and even worsen the prenatal changes that their body adopted during pregnancy well after giving birth.

I saw a new patient who'd been under care with another chiropractor before moving to our area. She'd brought up her hunchback type of appearance, noting that it had gotten worse over time, and said her former chiropractor told her that it was just the "mom back." Mom back is not a diagnosis and this is just more hand waving. Common does not mean normal. It is quite common that women demonstrate these dysfunctional postural changes after birth, but that doesn't mean it's normal for that to happen. I don't blame that doctor, but hopefully she's reading this book and understands that improving posture is possible.

If you search Upper Cross Syndrome or Lower Cross Syndrome, you'll find the work of Vladimir Janda and if you see pictures, you'll see what my patient's former chiropractor called "mom back."[2] It appears to me that this postural syndrome has worsened significantly with the increased use of handheld devices and computers. The more time you spend sitting slouched before a screen, the more likely you'll find yourself completely destroying all of the postural gains you've made in the past three chapters.

You can, of course, offset this by intentionally taking posture breaks from work and by being mindful of where your chin, tongue, rib cage, and tailbone are with regularity. I recommend to my patients that each time they compulsively check their phone, they also check those body parts.

One thing we haven't touched on is the position of your shoulders. When you bring your chin back so that your bowling ball is over your body, ideally your shoulders find themselves beside your body rather than in front of it. But maybe you've been walking around gorilla-style with your arms dangling *in front* of your torso. I am not calling you a gorilla, I just said you might sometimes look like one. And if you do, let's work on that.

If you have your chin and tongue in an appropriate posture, but your shoulders are still rounded forward, roll one shoulder at a time up, back, and down; repeat on the other side. Now your arms can rest beside you, and this gives us another checkpoint: where are your ears? If you've completed all of the previous steps (chin retraction, tip of your tongue to the roof of your closed mouth, shoulders individually rolled up/back/down to rest beside your body, and rib cage on top of pelvis), then from the side, your ears should be stacked on top of your newly-positioned shoulders. It's a whole new look!

If you've been gorilla-arming and emo-slouching for a while, this might be really hard to achieve. Repetition will be incredibly helpful in that regard, I promise. I also really do recommend you visit a chiropractor because having full joint motion within your spine makes achieving this neutral or centrated posture significantly easier. Most of my patients report feeling taller after their appointments, and I think it's just because they're actually able to stand taller with less effort after getting adjusted.

Perhaps you aren't gorilla-arming. Maybe instead you've been acutely aware of an upright posture and instead of rounding forward, you're doing the opposite: your rib cage is elevated, you're compulsively sucking in, and you actively pull your shoulders down and back at all times.

It's the opposite side of the same problem: this is not a centrated posture, either. To most people, it probably looks like "good posture" because you're more upright than your gorilla-armed counterparts. But the excess tension in the muscles you're using to create this over-corrected posture might actually be harder to retrain than simply strengthening the muscles that ought to actually be upholding your structure.

If you're an over-corrector, it's probably a bit more of a mental game, rather than just a physical one, to change your posture for the better. When I work with these patients, they immediately slouch into gorilla-arm posture as soon as I get them to relax their tightly-held abdomen (finally - after many bribes and much coercion). If they're not actively holding their ribcage up by sucking their abdomen in and therefore flaring their ribcage up (meaning we can see their ribs sticking out rather than lying flush with the rest of their abdomen under their breast tissue - sometimes I just call them "rib boobs" for simplicity), they immediately slouch.

Either of these positions (gorilla-arms or over-correction) necessitate breathing in an inefficient manner, which we addressed in the last chapter. So the over-correctors are actually the second level of dysfunction of the gorilla-arms. They've corrected their gorilla-arming ways and slouching emo kid appearance, but they haven't made the right correction: they've just created new tension.

The over-correctors have imbalances in the same muscle groups as the gorilla-arm gang, which are the same places mentioned in Upper and Lower Cross Syndromes. They look different, but they have a lot of the same tension. Sometimes the tension is caused by muscles that are long and tight (like stretched out and super tight upper traps from your bowling ball sitting away from your body) and sometimes the muscles are short and tight (like shortened upper trap muscles that are resting near your ears because you breathe with upward motion of your chest).

Instead of either scenario, I want you to actually have a really centrated posture and be able to maintain it. In the last chapter, our exercise was to work on breathing while lying down. Now we're going to bring you upright, though not fully yet. One step at a time. This will begin retraining your diaphragm for upright posture and will also help you connect with your pelvic floor. Both will help improve your posture, which will help improve your pelvic floor function.

Exercise - Perineal Palpation

Stand tall with your feet hip width apart in front of a bench or chair that is approximately the height of the bottom of your knee. Now we'll do a trick from Dr. Stuart McGill to introduce hip hinging: place the fingertips of your right hand on your sternum (bone in the center of your chest) and the fingertips of your left hand on your pubic symphysis (bony joint at the center of your pubic region). Now you have a marker for what your spinal position is. When you move your hips backward for this exercise, if your hands get closer together, you've rounded your spine (wrong); if your hands get further apart, you've extended your spine (wrong); if your hands stay the same distance apart, then you've moved at your hips (right).

So now, checking that your hands maintain their exact distance apart, send your hips backward and down until you find your ischial tuberosities (remember them from your vocab words? They're your "butt bones") on the bench. You're likely leaning a bit forward from your hip hinge, so go ahead and sit upright and keep your feet flat on the floor while still keeping your same hand position. If you're sitting on your tailbone instead of your ischial tuberosities, your hands will get closer together when you lean back to upright your spine. If your hands stayed the same distance apart, then you're now in a fairly neutral upright seated position.

If you find that you're slouching already, do that little chin tuck we talked about to bring your bowling ball on top of your body, and imagine a string pulling you upright from the top of the back of your head. If your shoulders are now tight because you over-corrected, fix this by shrugging one shoulder up, rolling it backward, then placing it down. Repeat on the opposite side. Now gently shake out your shoulders so they're not engaged.

Now notice if you have any tension in your abdomen. Gently poke it like we did in the last exercise and see if it's pliable or rigid. If it's pliable and you're still in an upright position, great: move on to the next part. If you have tension, try to coax yourself into letting it go, and reset the position as many times as you need to in order to achieve this neutral position without abdominal tension.

Those paragraphs were just the setup - we haven't even started the exercise yet - so hopefully that makes you realize how important that was. Now we're actually going to do the exercise.

Place your hands on your sides like you're doing an imitation of your third grade teacher about to scold that one kid who was smart enough to not sit still for eight hours a day. We did this in the last breathing exercise, so hopefully your thumbs are behind you and your hands are wrapped around your lower rib cage and abdomen.

With your mouth closed (of course), take a deep breath in and notice where your breath goes. Your lower abdomen and outsides of your rib cage ought to expand into your hands (including into your thumbs), and at the end of your inhale, your chest should expand as well, but not by moving upward toward the ceiling. Think expansion, not uprising, which is probably a crony capitalist mantra, but we're just talking breath.

On exhale, your rib cage will return to the starting position (not squeezing, just gently returning) and your abdomen will also deflate. I wish that I could use expand and contract like the antonyms that they are, but I think that might be where some of the misinterpretation comes from: people contract the muscles of their abdomen on exhale and end up creating excess tension. At the end of your exhale, your abdomen should still be relaxed.

The first part of the exercise is simply awareness. But given that I am pretty certain that your thumbs felt almost no expansion on inhale, I want you to gently rub your thumbs where they are along your back to create some more awareness of that area. Now, without creating excess tension in your abdomen, expand your breath into your thumbs on your next inhale. That felt different, didn't it? Another cue I give patients that came from Martina Ježková, a physiotherapist and DNS instructor, is to think of breathing into their kidneys. Spend a few breaths here. The exact same deflation should happen on exhale. No need to create tension during this exercise.

The final part of the exercise is going to involve you palpating your own perineum. Some people have the arm span of an albatross and can sit on their own hands with their hands facing upward, essentially cupping both of their ischial tuberosities ("butt bones") - meaning that their fingers are touching their perineum - without slouching. I am one of those people, so I was quite surprised when I started introducing this exercise to patients and found that my arms are apparently above-average length. Lots of people have to slump in order for them to sit on their hands. If you have albatross arms, go with the cupping of the ischial tuberosities version.

If you have normal length arms or short arms, you'll need to alter the setup a bit. The easiest way to do this is to put one hand under your butt crack with your palm up and fingers facing forward toward your pubic symphysis. Ideally, you can do this without having to hunch or bend in any way, and can just rotate your shoulders enough to get your hand in position, but still have your rib cage mostly stacked on top of your pelvis. Double-check that your feet are both still flat on the ground, and breathe normally. When I say that, I mean breathe as if breathing like we discussed in Chapter 2 was a normal endeavor for you.

Whether you are cupping your ischial tuberosities or sitting on your hand, you should feel your perineum lower into your fingers/hand on inhale, and feel it relax away from your hand on exhale. If you can't feel this, it might be that you need to practice your palpating skills (I'm actually not being a jerk), or it could mean that you are holding tension in your pelvic floor. We'll assume the latter because if it's the former, the practice comes from doing the thing. To get better at palpating, you need to palpate.

Let's practice your palpation and at the same time get better awareness of your pelvic floor. If you *don't* feel your perineum gently lowering into your hands, apply a bit more firm pressure from your fingertips. You probably have pants on (though I'm not judging if you don't), and I'm not talking about entering any orifices. I just want you to press gently into your perineum with your fingers or hand between your ischial tuberosities. I don't want you to *breathe* harder, I just want you to *feel* more firmly.

Sometimes this increase in pressure helps my patients to feel things better, but other times it helps give their brain the information about how much tension they have in their pelvic floor muscles because - even if they're not practiced in palpation - they can feel it from the outside.

Now can you feel your pelvic floor expanding into your hands on inhale and relaxing away from your hands on exhale? If not, you're a lost cause.

I'm kidding.

If not, this is the exact exercise I want you to do twice a day - when you get up in the morning and before you go to bed - until you can feel your pelvic floor moving in sync with your breath.

If you *can* feel your pelvic floor moving with your breath, I want you to revisit this exercise at least three times per week. It's a quick way to help bring your breath back into your core and out of your shoulders if you're feeling stressed.

These seated or perineum-palpating breathing exercises can replace a few of your four times per day breathing exercises that I know you haven't forgotten me recommending in Chapter 2. So you keep breathing, and now we're working on your posture, breath, and stress response all at the same time. Go, us.

CHAPTER 4

SILENT SUFFERING

In my practice, I observe how people are breathing when they come in. It's part of my initial exam with a new patient, but is also something I check on sort of without even meaning to. People are usually freaked out when they realize how much I'm observing when they think we're just hanging out being normal people doing whatever it is that normal people do. (I can't know. Apparently I'm not one. Apparently normal people are not doing breathing assessments and gait evaluations of their friends, so I'm told.)

When I'm with a patient, I'm totally present with their body and their energy while we check in and they update me on how their life has been since I last saw them. Most of that is easily identifiable in their breathing patterns. Are they taking shallow, rapid breaths? Short, gasping ones? Do they breathe through their nose or their mouth? Are their shoulders rising as they inhale? Are their traps super bulky? Are they clenching their jaw?

All of those questions give clues as to what the patient might not be telling me verbally, but are incredibly important in their care because their shallow breaths tell me that their nervous system senses stress, even if they don't feel it or report it. Their tight traps and their rising shoulders tell me their diaphragm isn't driving the breathing pattern.

Sometimes just pointing out these places of tension can help release them. I took a Neurolinguistic Programming training (which can be either very cool or super manipulative) and one of my favorite takeaways from the course was the line:

Awareness brings choice. Choice is better than no choice.

Drawing awareness to tightness in your shoulders usually helps to remind you that you have the choice to relax your shoulders instead of holding them rigidly. You might not have realized that you were holding them so tensely until someone brought it to your attention, but then you can choose what to do next.

But if you're habitually raising your shoulders to breathe and breathing through your mouth, it's going to take a lot longer to rehabilitate your pelvic floor because the health of the pelvic floor is dependent on the health of the entire core.

(Hopefully you're starting to see where the first few chapters laid the foundation for us. If not, there are no refunds on the book, but perhaps you can hawk it on ebay.)

And then I need to ask the right questions. With new patients, we ask three times about pelvic floor dysfunction. Most doctors ask about incontinence because it's a "red flag" question. If you've all of a sudden started losing control of your bladder or your bowels, that's a red flag and we need to emergently figure out why. But alongside that question, we add a note that says "including stress incontinence" so that it opens up the conversation.

We also have a checkbox section on our new patient paperwork that offers specific examples of pelvic floor dysfunction that they can simply put a check mark in if it applies to them - stress incontinence, urge incontinence, bowel incontinence, overactive bladder, painful intercourse, lack of orgasm, hemorrhoids.

The third way is that we ask them out loud about those questions. Sometimes people say "no" to the first question and don't check a single box. I typically ask directly, "Can you run, jump, cough, laugh, and sneeze without leaking any amount of urine?" That's usually when we get the ball rolling on more conversation, but it does often come with several caveats. Some examples:

- I *can*, but if I've had too much water before a work-out, I might just go to the bathroom first and then I should be fine.
- I probably would if I did any jump rope, but I just avoid that.
- No, because I've used a pessary since my oldest was born.
- Yeah, but it's not ever enough to have to change my pants.
- Yes, but I just wear dark leggings because it's not a lot.

It's a great opportunity to begin unwinding the untruths that women have been told, and start educating about what's really possible with pelvic floor rehabilitation.

Sometimes they say yes but get a little dodgy about it, then I'll ask if they can go to a trampoline park on a full bladder with no issues. Often if I'm suspecting PFD, the response to that question is "Well..." and then we can have further conversations.

Sometimes people say that they *can* run, jump, cough, sneeze, and laugh without any leaking. These people do exist, despite what you may have heard from hand-waving friends and relatives. I personally need to make sure that I'm thorough in my questioning so that my patients understand the importance of reporting these symptoms if they do come up. Maybe it will come up later in care after we've established a rapport, or when new symptoms arise, or maybe they'll just be able to tell their friend who laughs off having to go to the bathroom before her bootcamp workout that doing so is neither normal nor funny.

The other part about asking these questions is that they aren't one-time questions. Yes, we ask these questions in our new patient intake, but that leaves the door open for us to ask them frequently. Maybe the patient will never have a single instance of pelvic floor dysfunction in her lifetime (or however long she sees us for care), but if she does, I don't want it to go under the radar. When a patient has a new complaint or a new life change, I make a point to ask about her pelvic floor, even if it doesn't seem related.

You have a new case of tennis elbow after playing in a pickleball tournament? How's your pelvic floor these days?

Oh, you're moving to a new house? How's your pelvic floor?

One of the most meaningful times I check in on the pelvic floor is if the life change they report involves them grieving in some way.

Grief is something that is often accompanied by pelvic floor dysfunction, and I don't even have to speculate why. Grief is a form of stress, and we've talked about stress and what it does to your body. There's also the energetic component of your root chakra (your energy center that gives you a sense of security and groundedness, which perhaps not-so-coincidentally is located at the pelvic floor), and yogis will often point to a blocked first chakra in those with PFD.

If talking about invisible energy is too much for you (I will point you toward x-rays, cell phone communication, sonar, and radar to prove its existence, but I know that some people still think that chakras are a load of hogwash), then what about the adage of "the bottom dropping out?"

When we lose something or someone or a belief or an identity, it often feels like the bottom of whatever we were just standing on completely dropped out. And what's on the bottom of our torso? Our pelvic floor.

It's a stretch to say that grief *causes* pelvic floor dysfunction, but I have seen many grieving people present with a new or returned onset of PFD after a grief-inducing event.

I experienced this personally while writing this book, actually. Mary, my friend and Back Office Manager (whom

I'll reference in Chapter 9), was shot and killed while walking her dog, just over two weeks before her wedding day. She left the office, went home, and I never saw her again. The shooter claimed five victims' lives that day, senselessly disrupting thousands of others.

I have a general practice of breathwork, movement, nutrition, and meditation techniques that I utilize in a fairly ongoing manner, and I continued those in the aftermath. But grief and the absolute shock of losing Mary in this way hit quite hard. In addition to losing my friend and grieving for her fiancé, family, my staff, and our practice community, I also lost my right-hand woman for my practice. Talk about the bottom dropping out.

I experienced symptoms on the day of her Celebration of Life (which was initially supposed to be her wedding day and our shared anniversary). Her fiancé and parents asked those of us who were going to attend her wedding to wear what we'd planned for the wedding to her Celebration of Life. I knew the dress I was going to wear, and the morning of, I decided that since this was a very special occasion, I would don a pair of heels to kick the outfit up a notch.

You can probably guess from reading this book that I don't take wearing heels lightly: for good reason. Heels create a forward shift in your center of gravity, meaning your heel-wearing posture is akin to a pregnant posture. I therefore reserve heels for special occasions - like this one. I'd helped set up her wedding dress to be on display and carried a few plants and flowers, but nothing I did that day (aside from walking in heels) was at all strenuous. I took my heels off on my way home and was actually just sitting comfortably with some friends, sharing memories of Mary, when I felt some irritation consistent with hemorrhoids.

Hemorrhoids and I go way back, and I've written about that on my Substack before. But I'd not had any symptoms in quite a while: the last time I remember having a truly inflamed hemorrhoid, I was pregnant with my youngest (he's 6).

To have those symptoms show up when I wasn't straining for a bowel movement or doing anything at all truly points me toward grief-related pelvic floor dysfunction. Maybe it's a self-fulfilling prophecy, or maybe I would've been fine if I hadn't added the extra layer of stress of wearing the heels. Maybe the heels didn't change anything but how good my outfit looked. Regardless, the bottom dropped out and my pelvic floor responded.

Luckily, I have a few tricks for that. Some homeopathic suppositories (which I personally recommend using just before bed and not before a day of activity; just trust me on this one), plus pelvic floor relaxation techniques and exercises I'm giving you in this book, and my hemorrhoids went from inflamed and painful to negligible in under five days.

Just like any other previously injured area of the body, there is a potential of relapsing symptoms in the pelvic floor. I treat relapses similarly to new occurrences of dysfunction, but keep the patient history in mind. The same strategies that help an injury can help a re-injury.

Even if there's not a grief-related event, I still frequently check in on pelvic floor function simply because research has shown us how under-reported these symptoms are. In a 2018 poll, women aged 50-80 were asked about incontinence. Of the women polled who were under 65, 43% reported incontinence; over 65, that number was 51%. Two-thirds of those women had not talked to their doctor about their symptoms, but many reported that their incontinence was happening daily and was disruptive to their life.[1]

Maybe they don't report their symptoms because they think nothing can be done; maybe it's because they're embarrassed. The poll didn't specify *why* these women weren't talking to their providers about this health issue, but the fact remains: they are suffering in silence. It's possible that some of my patients will choose to lie about their symptoms, but at least the conversation has been started.

If you've experienced incontinence, tell your doctor: not just your primary care physician or your OB. Tell any practitioner who is examining you or putting their hands on you. Maybe you'll get some hand-waving, but at least it'll be part of your medical history and maybe if your provider hears about these symptoms enough from enough patients, they'll investigate ways to help their patients (or maybe you could gift them this book as a very non-subtle hint that they have some things to learn).

If you're embarrassed about having this conversation, I get it. It is not the most fun thing to admit that beyond potty training, you've wet your pants. It likely feels even more embarrassing if you are admitting to fecal incontinence (pooping your pants). But this is such a crucial piece of information for your doctor to know about your overall function. As I stated before, recent incontinence is a "red flag" question that in most doctor's offices is a checkbox that you can either say "yes" or "no" to. That's because there are serious conditions (like cauda equina syndrome or other spinal cord injury) that require immediate emergency care. But just because this isn't an emergency doesn't mean it doesn't require attention.

Exercise - Upright Breath & Box Breathing

Now's a great time to practice uprighting your spine. We practiced breathing while lying down, then while seated, and now we're going to do it while standing. You're going to do the exact same setup as before, which I'll detail for you in a second so you don't have to find it.

But first, I am going to make a plug for a simple but powerful tool to help you with your breathing practice called the Core 360 Belt. Erin McGuire, PT, OCS, designed the belt to help support her patients and the design was so impactful that she started selling the belts to other practitioners and to anyone who was looking to improve their breathing.

I love them, wear one for feedback during exercise when I want some extra attention, and sell them in my office to help patients in their at-home exercises. You can go to core360belt.com to get yours (and use the code "mumma" at checkout to get a discount).

The Core 360 Belt is the antithesis of a waist trainer. Not only are you intentionally expanding your abdomen, but this is something that fits around your waist that encourages you to do so. There are a few different versions of the belt, but the original belt is helpful for most people to get adequate feedback of their breathing pattern and encourage better expansion.

If you have a Core 360 Belt already, that's awesome. Grab it and put it on. If you don't, you can either place your hands on your sides for feedback sporadically throughout the exercise or you can put a small elastic band (think one that is about 10-12 inches in diameter, but can stretch to at least 18-24 inches in diameter easily) around your waist to try to get some amount of feedback (though it won't be nearly as effective as the belt). Don't use a leather belt or anything that's rigid because you want feedback without compression.

Stand tall with your feet hip width apart. If you're not barefoot, now is a great time to kick off your shoes. Most shoes tend to create a change in your center of gravity and distribute your weight differently than standing on your own two feet. Most shoes also compress your toes so that the ball of your foot is wider than your toes, which is not the shape of a foot that hasn't been compressed by shoes. Set those piggies free!

Wiggle your toes and splay them out so that you have a good base of support. Check in with your own center of gravity. Lean forward and backward to get a feel for where you feel the most balanced or centrated.

Keeping a neutral neck position (bowling ball on top of body, tongue on the roof of your mouth), do the single-sided shoulder roll that we've done before: roll one shoulder at a time up, back, and down; repeat on the other side.

Now notice if you have any tension in your abdomen. If not, great. If you do, jiggle your belly gently with a hand to convince yourself that you're safe enough to relax your abdomen. Now you're upright and ideally in a comfortable standing position and we'll start some box breathing.

Do all of the following through your nose, including the exhales. Breathe in for a five count, hold your breath for a five count, exhale for a five count, and hold that for a five count. If you can easily complete that, you can increase the size of the "box" by increasing your count: inhale for six, hold six, exhale six, hold six, for example.

If you can't easily complete that, no problem. Keep playing around with five counts. Check your shoulders to make sure you're not elevating them or raising your chest to accomplish this task. The point is to practice breathing fully while standing and also to increase your conscious control over your diaphragm.

I've played around with box breathing for a while; 22 is the biggest box I have built so far, and that was hard. I have a feeling that some monks, practiced yogis, or free divers would have no problem with 22, but the majority of people I work with struggle with a box of ten. At the same time, I've yet to work with someone who wasn't able to increase the size of their box breathing simply by practicing box breathing.

Most people seem to be able to get to 12 or 15 by practicing once per day. That's what I recommend you do: practice one box breath each day.

If you're keeping up with your four sessions of breathing each day that I recommended in Chapter 2, you may have added perineal palpation for one of those and you can add box breathing for another session. It can be a great option for a meditation session to build a breathing box.

PART 2

THE PROBLEMS

CHAPTER 5

LEAKING - IT'S ACTUALLY NOT OKAY TO PEE YOUR PANTS

We've talked about basic function and anatomy of the pelvic floor, the importance of breathing and posture for establishing normal pelvic floor function, and how to talk to your doctor (or how to ask your patients if *you're* the doctor). Now let's talk about what dysfunction looks like.

It's not surprising how prevalent pelvic floor dysfunction is when you realize the amount of hand waving that occurs in response to its reporting. Peeing your pants is seen as a rite of passage. Once you've reached a certain state (pregnancy) or a certain milestone (birth) or a certain age (menopausal), then you're just expected to pee your pants a little. And if you insist on a different outcome, you'll have a hand waved toward you to indicate that you should move on.

But some of us aren't willing to move on.

Some of us are plagued with a variety of dysfunctions that we're not willing to accept as our new normal. Some of us have expectations of healing, function, and normalcy, both inside our drawers and out. Some of us wish to remain continent (as in the opposite of *in*continent, meaning that we are able to hold our urine and not that we're a land mass).

A personal note

I say "us" because I am one of the women who was plagued by pelvic floor dysfunction. And in one of those cosmic jokes, it wasn't what got me so passionate about working with the pelvic floor.

Nope, I was already telling women that they didn't need to pee their pants because I knew it to be true. I'd experienced 40 weeks and three days of pregnancy, a 40 hour labor, and a vaginal birth, and I never peed my pants. After some initial rehab (not enough by my current standards, honestly), I returned to fairly high intensity of physical activity and fitness after having my first baby (including PRing my deadlift at 293 pounds - maybe I'm bragging or maybe I'm just pointing out that that's a lot of pressure on one's pelvic floor: you decide) and still didn't pee my pants.

And *then*, over two years later, I started to experience pelvic floor dysfunction in my second pregnancy, but it went largely unnoticed because one of the truths that is actually appropriate to hand wave is that you will have increased urine output during pregnancy. I was experiencing bladder spasms, but because bladder spasms cause the detrusor muscle of the bladder to contract, the result of a spasm is the urge to go to the bathroom more frequently.

During pregnancy, there is a normal increase in the need to go to the bathroom more frequently, so detecting overactive bladder (OAB) or bladder spasms can be tricky.

I do not have evidence for this next line (it is merely based on my experience personally and as a doctor); if you get up more than twice per night to go to the bathroom, there is something else going on. It may be a chemical or food sensitivity, a symptom of low back pain, or related more to mental and emotional health than the bladder itself. Even during pregnancy.

I've written about my experience before on lindsaymumma.substack.com, so I'll just share the condensed version of my story: I started to get bladder spasms at the beginning of my second pregnancy, which are lowest on the list of common pelvic floor dysfunctions. This was concurrent with moving into our new home, which we later discovered had some fairly high EMF exposure and some "dirty" electricity; these may have been a contributing factor, but I can't say for sure.

Bladder spasms are sometimes a symptom associated with interstitial cystitis, which is an autoimmune condition wherein the lining of the bladder is inflamed persistently, but they rarely exist on their own. Unless, of course, you're a person who's been talking about how pelvic floors need to function optimally all of the time. Then the Universe squeezes your bladder throughout the day to see how you'll handle it. I digress. The point is that I could sneeze, jump, or cough without any bladder leakage, but then occasionally I'd get a bladder spasm that would cause leakage. It's been quite the journey to have a healthy, fully functioning pelvic floor. This book is not about *my* pelvic floor journey; just know that I've been through the ringer on pelvic floor therapies and modalities, so part of what I teach has come from what I've learned personally. Back to the subject matter at hand.

Naming Pelvic Floor Dysfunction

Let's talk about the things that can go wrong with pelvic floors and what symptoms might arise if yours isn't working optimally.

Pelvic floor dysfunction (PFD) refers to any of the following symptoms (either alone or in combination). This is like Irritable Bowel Syndrome, where you go to your doctor and tell them that you're experiencing irritability of your bowels and then you get diagnosed with Irritable Bowel Syndrome. So if you have dysfunction in your pelvic floor, you will be diagnosed with pelvic floor dysfunction. And now I've de-mystified all of healthcare for you. You're welcome.

- **Stress urinary incontinence (SUI)** is the most common pelvic floor dysfunction and affects a reported one in four women. As we've discussed, a lot of women aren't reporting their symptoms (and many of those who *are* have been given a lot of hand waving as a response). This means that when the bladder or pelvic cavity is stressed (such as with a sneeze or jumping), urine leaks out of the urethra.

- **Bowel Incontinence** is similar to stress urinary incontinence, but significantly more disruptive to people who experience this type of incontinence. Rather than the urethra leaking urine, the anus leaks feces. The comical version of this is a shart, but there's not really anything funny about pooping your pants.

- **Overactive bladder (OAB)** is when you're using the bathroom typically more than eight times per day. If you think of it in terms of a day's length, that's more frequent than once every two hours. It's also characterized by the sudden onset of the need to go to the bathroom, often when the bladder is not actually full.

- **Urge Incontinence** sometimes accompanies OAB in that when the sudden need to urinate comes about, there is immediate leaking. In essence, the urgency causes the leaking rather than a stress to the bladder.

- **Pelvic organ prolapse (POP)** refers to a descent of the organs within the pelvis (such as the bladder, rectum, or uterus) further into (or out of) the pelvic cavity.

Additional symptoms

- **Pelvic pain (or pelvic girdle pain)** is not always as a result of pelvic floor dysfunction, but is a symptom in the same region as the pelvic floor and can also contribute to additional PFD. Pain within the pelvic region can be as a result of lack of motion in the hip joints, SI joints, or spine, and can also be a result of referral from trigger points, fascial tension, or organs.

- **Coccydynia** literally translates to coccyx pain. Pain in your tailbone falls under "pelvic pain" but is also categorized as its own entity. It can be caused by or be the cause of other PFD symptoms.

- **Dyspareunia** is the official term for painful intercourse.

- **Vulvodynia** is the term for chronic vulvar pain (remember that this is the external female genitalia).

- **Hemorrhoids** are anal blood vessels, but they can become enlarged or inflamed or even thrombose. Colloquially we tend to call hemorrhoid disease "hemorrhoids" the same way that a lot of people say that they have TMJ when they mean TMD. Hemorrhoids themselves are normal, but when they're inflamed, the anus can become itchy or painful and there may be visible blood in the stool due to bleeding. Sometimes a hemorrhoid extrudes outside of the anus and can be reduced by pushing it back in, but sometimes it becomes more severely extruded and cannot be pushed back in.

- **Anorgasmia** is the inability to achieve an orgasm despite adequate stimulation. This is another one of those multifactorial issues that can contribute to other pelvic floor dysfunction (such as increased tension in fascia or muscles) or be related to mental and emotional health, previous trauma, or other factors.

All of the aforementioned are signs of PFD and are *not* normal. Some are more common than others, but common is not the same as normal. Common means something happens frequently. Normal means that it is physiologically appropriate. It is not physiologically appropriate to pee your pants, have pain, or have parts of your body descending to where they don't belong.

I don't care how many of your friends or family have the same symptoms: this just means that the symptoms are common; they're still not normal.

But What About Pregnancy?

Listen. Or read, or whatever. Check your watch and the length of the rest of this chapter and consider your reading speed. If you don't think you'll finish the rest of this chapter right now, then I'll ask you to set the book down. If you need a break before you move on, go take one. But this part of the chapter should be read in one sitting. So if you need to lock some doors or pretend you're sleeping or otherwise create a diversion so that you can complete this chapter, please do so. There are no stopping points. It's like a stream of consciousness that you're being carried along in a boat. Maybe I'm even using this imagery because of that whole boat theory of the pelvic floor that we talked about earlier. But if you get off the boat in the middle of the stream, it's going to turn into the really creepy ride in the first Willy Wonka movie and things just won't make sense. Stay in the boat. Here we go.

It's actually not okay to pee your pants when you're pregnant. I know I just made at least one reader make an embarrassing face of disgust or anger because *how dare I* say something so blasphemous when it wasn't at all her fault that she peed during her pregnancy. I know this reaction exists because of how many times I've had this conversation in real life, or IRL as the cool kids say. (Am I too far behind? Are the TikTokkers not saying IRL? It doesn't matter). If I spoke directly to this one reader who read what I stated and defensively responded with how she did *everything* she could and did *everything* right and she *still* peed her pants, so sometimes people just pee their pants and I should cut them some slack; I would vehemently disagree. Here's what I would say:

"I understand how hard you worked and how frustrating it was to just discover that what you'd been told - that peeing your pants was a normal part of pregnancy and a rite of passage of sorts for new moms; that if you just wear a panty liner, that'll take care of it, and maybe get fitted for a pessary if you need to, but for the most part women just deal with it so join the club - was a load of malarkey. I get it. I would bristle, too. But instead of getting bristly, it's possible that you could stop the lies in their tracks, try something different, and then spread the word about how peeing your pants isn't normal."

(I'd probably also say the rest of the contents of this chapter because brevity is not my forte, but I won't include it in quotes.)

I can hear the pushback now (because I've heard it so many times). Yes, I *do* understand the physical demands of pregnancy, the physiological changes that the body goes through (which I already outlined in Chapter 3), and the increased load on the pelvic floor with simultaneous increased relaxation of ligaments and muscles as a result of a cascade of hormonal changes; the increase in blood volume and cardiac output and sweat production and how everything not only looks different but feels different and sometimes even smells different and how absolutely strange and bizarre it is to fathom that a person could come out of another person unscathed and then go on to create more people in a forever-running Russian doll situation of sorts. I get it.

And yet. There are plenty of women who experience pregnancies - multiple of them - without ever leaking urine. They don't "get" the joke of being unsure whether their water broke or whether they peed themselves at the end of pregnancy. They don't run to the bathroom before their prenatal workout. They don't cross their legs when they laugh, cough, or sneeze. They're in the Motherhood Club, but they're not in the sub-section of the Motherhood Club that includes the women who joke about the aforementioned, often in an omniscient way, as if to suggest that if those other mothers who don't *yet* pee their pants are going to find out one day soon enough just what it *really* means to be a mother. And how it means sacrificing your underwear right alongside your solo bathroom trips. How it means that you'll never be the same *down there.*

Rather than get angry at the women who think they know better, let's understand that they've been told the malarkey, too. They've been given the "this is just part of it" speech, maybe even by their doctor, and been told that they'll have to suck it up (and suck it in) just like the rest of us, and nothing they do can make it any better.

Unless, of course, you ask your neighbor Janice, who had pelvic reconstruction surgery and thinks *you should, too, and it's not that bad of a recovery, honestly. And if you get a hysterectomy at the same time - who needs hormones, anyway? - it's way easier,* says Janice as she sips from her glass of red. (We'll talk about surgery later.)

Back to the point (though I really can take those tangents for a nice run, can't I?), pregnancy is not a reason to pee your pants. It's often blamed as a reason, and there certainly are parts about the physiological changes of pregnancy and the demands of labor, birthing, and recovery that would lend themselves toward your propensity to tinkle just a bit when you didn't mean to.

The book is called *Your Pelvic Floor Sucks*, so it's not like you expected me to be all warm and cuddly about this. But I'm not blaming you if you pee your pants. (And if you took Janice's advice and got all of your female sex organs removed and had mesh implanted to save your pelvic floor and now you wish you'd read this book before I'd written it and before you did that: I understand why you made that choice.) I'm simply going to tell you, dear reader who is offended that I didn't even give you the grace of allowing you to wet yourself while pregnant, that peeing yourself is not normal, no matter why or when it happens.

I know, I'm a complete jerk.

But I'm also here to help.

Testimonial

When I met Dr. Lindsay Mumma, she educated me on the importance of diaphragmatic breathing. Inhaling slowly and deeply through the nose and gently pulling the air down to the belly. I felt expansion and strength in my low back and a stronger connection to my pelvic floor. In addition to relearning how to breathe properly, she recommended I do Postpartum Rehab. I smirked at this since it had been over 8 years since delivering my fifth child. But after multiple injuries to my back (and still peeing on myself) I thought, "Why not? Nothing else seems to be working long term." Over the course of 6 months of real intentional breathing and partaking in the rehab course, I noticed that not only had my back issues dissipated, but I was also able to go running without peeing on myself!

It turns out that the strength of the diaphragm is directly connected to the strength of the pelvic floor. Breathe correctly and feel the body regain internal strength. Nearly two years later I still practice exercises from Postpartum Rehab as well as the Functional Progression. This protocol is not necessarily a quick fix, but as Dr. Mumma reminds me "Slow is fast and fast is slow."

I'm happy to report that I've been able to make a full return to triathlon and am so happy to run whenever I feel like it. When you find your breath, you find your strength.

*- **Caroline K, 47***

Exercise - Hip Hinging to a Box

If you have a Core 360 Belt, grab it. If not, make do with your hands or an elastic band around your waist to get some feedback. We're going to practice hip hinging. We did this in the exercise from Chapter 3 just to get you set up for perineal palpation, but we're going to repetitively practice hip hinging to a box and coming back up. This is honestly a pretty big risk to go over in book form because my preference is to use visual, auditory, and tactile cues when working with patients, and I often find that a combination of all three are necessary. But a hip hinge is a crucial movement, and doing this exercise can help you strengthen your pelvic stabilizing muscles, so let's try.

The first thing I want you to think of is an example that my friend and colleague, Dr. Josh Satterlee, uses to instruct the hip hinge: picture yourself holding a tray of drinks that you've just picked up for your office from Starbucks, plus your own hot drink in your other hand. Now you have to open the door using your booty because your hands are full. The way you stick your butt behind you is most likely going to be a hip hinge.

The only problem with this example is that sometimes people will arch their back while doing this movement. So you can set your hypothetical coffees and lattes down and place your hand on your sternum and another on your pubic symphysis so that you could bump the door open with your backside while still keeping a neutral spinal position. Remember: if your hands get closer together or further apart between your sternum and your pubic symphysis, you've moved through your spine instead of around your hips and are doing the movement incorrectly; if they stay the same distance apart, you're doing the movement correctly. Now you're hip hinging. (It's called a hip hinge because you're moving around your hip joint as if it was a simple door hinge rather than a ball and socket joint.)

Now we're going to repeat the hip hinge, but use the movement to get you to a seated position. Stand in front of a bench or chair that is approximately the height of the bottom of your knee, just like you did before when you practiced breathing while seated. Ideally, you don't have shoes on so that your feet have a sense of the ground beneath you. Use your hands on your sternum and your pubic symphysis again so that you can move around your hips rather than bending your spine.

Ensure that your hands maintain their exact distance apart while you send your hips backward and then once you can't send your hips any further back, allow your knees to bend as you move your hips down toward the bench until you find your ischial tuberosities (butt bones) on the bench behind you. Your knees should not have come forward at all, but should still be stacked over top of your ankles. Once your butt bones hit the bench, press your feet into the ground to return to standing. Keep your knees facing forward so that they do not cave in toward each other. You may need to release your hands from your sternum and pubic symphysis and hold them out in front of you to help with maintaining balance, but ensure that you keep your torso in the same position and don't bend around your spine.

The movement to return to standing from sitting is not going to mimic the movement going down. We're essentially creating a hip hinge on the way down, but coming out of the seated position in what would be closer to the return position from a squat. A hip hinge is what you do when performing a deadlift. A squat is what you do when performing - you guessed it - a squat. These are different movements that many exercisers tend to confuse and weirdly mix together if they've not had formal coaching.

My purpose for introducing this exercise to you is so that you can get comfortable with a hip hinge movement with something behind you so that you don't fall over. And you can also get comfortable with returning to a standing position from a squat with a base of support underneath you. Both of these will help you build strength, stability, and ultimately a sense of trust in your pelvic floor.

Common Faults

Assuming you do the hip hinge part correctly - you will; I believe in you - there are some common faults when coming up out of the seated position.

- The most common way people mess up this exercise is by losing their spinal position, but you won't do that because you've got your handy dandy hands on your sternum and pubic symphysis to help guide you, so you won't arch or round your back on your way back up (arching would be way more common than rounding).

- The next way is to have their knees cave toward each other. I already told you not to do that, so hopefully you're not. But to safeguard, it might be helpful to take one of those elastic bands that you may have used for feedback until you got a Core 360 Belt and loop it around your knees so that you actually end up cueing yourself to keep your knees gently pressed outward into the band. You don't need to stretch the band; just meet its resistance.

- One incredibly common fault is to lose your neck position. Many people jut their chin forward rather than keeping their bowling ball on top of their body. (Should I start referring to your bowling ball as your head again, or should I just stick with "bowling ball?")

- The other common fault is that people will actually try to reverse the movement when they come back up from the seated position. But because of the levers of your thighs and the weight of your torso, it's pretty freaking hard to accomplish this in general. When your pelvic floor is dysfunctional, that task becomes nigh impossible without significant amounts of compensation.

- Finally, a lot of people hoist themselves off of the bench that they're seated on, using momentum to propel them upward rather than primarily relying on their glute (butt) muscles to do the work for them.

Steer clear of the faults. If you are completely new to hip hinging, I don't recommend doing more than two sets of ten repetitions with at least a minute rest in between sets. Do this twice per week. If this is something you're familiar with, then grooving the pattern to ensure you maintain appropriate spinal positioning and that you're driving out of the bottom position with your glutes is a great warm-up or accessory exercise to tack on to your workout. Try 3x10 with intention two or three times per week.

CHAPTER 6

TRIGGER POINTS

If your pelvis hurts, it's hard to have normal function. This is true of just about any part of the body. Pain causes inflammation (and inflammation causes pain), so an area that's in pain is already not functioning normally because the physiology of the area is different.

If you've ever had pain anywhere in your body, you know that the typical response is to hold it tight. This is a great short-term strategy, but over a long period of time, tightness can lead to more pain. If you consistently hold tension in a muscle, you'll end up with trigger points. Trigger points are palpable nodules that show up within a muscle as a result of persistent contracture of that muscle. They can show up even if you've not had any pain just because you're holding tension in a muscle. Trigger points within the pelvic floor are incredibly common. We know all about trigger points because of an incredible woman, Dr. Janet Travell. Fun fact for your trivia bank: she was the very first female White House physician.

Trigger points can be active or latent. Active trigger points will actively cause pain without provocation and can also refer pain to other areas of the body. Latent trigger points won't be painful unless you poke them. The complicating part about that is that Professor Kolar, the founder of Dynamic Neuromuscular Stabilization, says that while trigger points may present in the body, they actually exist in the brain. If there is a trigger point that's showing up, it's not just because a muscle is tight: it's because the brain has told that muscle that being tight is the best option.

If we address *why* a muscle is tight, then we can get the trigger point to release itself because the brain can send the message that it's not necessary to hold that tension any longer. If not, we have tools within manual therapy that help us to release trigger points: dry needling is one of my favorites, but other soft tissue techniques, adjustments, and even exercise can help us release trigger points as well.

Dr. Brett Winchester (he gave us the appropriate times for sucking in earlier in the book and is a DNS instructor) used to be the team doctor for the St. Louis Cardinals. He shared that he would often find a trigger point in the pec muscle that was present in throwers who had some trouble stabilizing their shoulder blade. Whenever they'd get the player's shoulder blade to better stabilize, the trigger point would be gone without them having directly treated the trigger point. He hypothesized that to "treat" the trigger point rather than the underlying reason why the trigger point was present would leave the player at greater risk of injury.

Another mentor of mine and DNS instructor is Robert Lardner, PT. Robert uses trigger points as check-ins with patients, which is a practice I've taken up as well. It's one thing to ask a patient how they've improved or not, but it's another entirely to hear from their body that they are doing better or that they're still struggling to improve. Trigger points are evidence of how the body is doing. A patient may think they haven't improved much because they still have pain, but if their brain is feeling more stability in an area, it will release trigger points, so we will find less of them on examination. Another patient may feel great, but examination shows us that latent trigger points are still present and we have some work to do.

For alleviating trigger points within the pelvic floor, pelvic health physical therapists (sometimes called pelvic PTs) and some chiropractors perform internal pelvic floor manual therapy and can help alleviate trigger points. These providers can utilize a gloved hand, internal biofeedback sensors, or manual therapy tools to help alleviate internal trigger points. One chiropractic study showed improvements in urinary incontinence after ischemic compression was applied to trigger points over the bladder, meaning that helpful work can also be done externally.[1] While I recommend working with a professional, this is also possible to do yourself.

Using a pelvic wand (which just looks like a sex toy if anyone is checking your search history at work) can be helpful both for identifying and alleviating internal trigger points. Sometimes this is more approachable to people than using their own hand, but your hand is one of the best tools you have available for alleviating a trigger point. Sometimes the location and angle of an internal trigger point can make the work challenging, which is where a wand can come in handy (pun absolutely intended).

As we discussed, dyspareunia is painful sex. Given what we've said about latent trigger points being nonpainful until they're poked, it makes sense that trigger points are often a component of this condition. Some people experience an increase in pain during intercourse, but some people have no pelvic pain until intercourse, at which point they begin to experience pain. Troubleshooting dyspareunia can be challenging because there are often emotional and mental components to this painful presentation because of the challenges it poses for intimacy in relationships as well as the energetic aspect of the root and sacral chakras. Also note that while dyspareunia is technically the name for painful intercourse, there can be pain with any penetration into the vagina.

Keep the multifactorial nature of dyspareunia in mind, but from a physical standpoint, pain that presents upon insertion is typically caused by tension in the outermost layer of the pelvic floor and can be linked to tension specifically within scar tissue in the perineum if it's present. Pain that presents during penetration is often related to internal trigger points or tension, or can be related to pelvic organ prolapse or other organ referral.

If painful intercourse does not improve with manual release of tension within the pelvic floor (combined with the exercises you're learning in this book), it's a great idea to get a good team together. We'll talk more about that in Chapter 15 when I address establishing a care team.

Exercise - Trigger Point Release

Let's start with your upper traps so that you can practice a trigger point release in an area that's easily accessible. Since we've already worked for several chapters to improve your breathing pattern, any remaining trigger points you have in these muscles can be easily released because the brain ought to be ready to let go of them. A simple strategy for alleviating a trigger point is ischemic compression.[2] That translates to pressing on something to decrease blood flow to the area.

Palpate your upper traps using one or two fingers to press with a firm pressure and feel around until you find a trigger point, which feels like a small nodule of tight muscle. Palpation is a skill that many people do not practice, but the benefit of trigger points is that they hurt, so if you poke one, you'll feel it internally, which can help you identify what you're feeling. Active trigger points will hurt worse and recreate referral pain (pain that is being experienced elsewhere in the body); latent trigger points will be tender when you touch them, but it doesn't really matter right now whether we're dealing with an active or latent trigger point. I just want you to find one in your upper traps because I'm fairly certain that you'll be able to locate one.

Once you locate a trigger point, press a bit harder into it. This will cause pain. If it doesn't, that's not a trigger point. Back off the pressure until you feel only pressure but not pain.

Maintain this level of pressure for about 20 or 30 seconds. Intentionally slow your breathing to induce more relaxation and send the message from your brain to your trigger point that you wish to release and relax that area while maintaining pressure on the trigger point. Repeating a mantra of "I am relaxed and release tension" or something similar can be helpful.

Don't release your pressure. After 20-30 seconds, you'll find that you will be able to apply more pressure to the trigger point without inducing pain. Apply more pressure, and then repeat the process (firm but non-painful pressure for 20-30 seconds with intentional slow breathing and relaxing thoughts followed by increasing the pressure in the area of the trigger point) a few more times. After about 90 seconds, the trigger point will most likely be gone.

Practiced hands will feel the trigger point "melt," which is the best word to describe the feeling of the trigger point relaxing. Un-practiced hands will simply note that it's no longer tender to poke the area. If it's not, don't keep poking at it. Give your brain and the trigger point some rest. Repeatedly attempting to release a trigger point can aggravate it further or send a signal to the brain that it should return the tension you just released because there's an injury in the area. Bring your focus back to the other exercises I've covered and try again another day.

After a trigger point release or attempted release, it can be helpful to stretch the area. If you worked on a trigger point in your right trap, lean your head to the left until you feel a gentle stretch in your right upper trap. It can be helpful to pull your head a little further to the left by placing your left hand on the right side of your head and applying gentle pressure toward the left. I've used the word gentle several times because I don't want you cranking on your neck. Hold this gentle stretch for two slow breaths and then release. Shake out your shoulders and palpate your right trap again. Even to un-practiced hands, you will likely be able to feel the difference after this brief and simple intervention.

Let's apply the same simple self-treatment to your pelvic floor. Using a clean hand, palpate your external and internal tissues. If you have a pelvic wand, feel free to use that instead of or in addition to your hand. Keep hygiene in mind: do not palpate into or around your anus and then bring that hand or wand into your vagina. When you do find trigger points, you can apply the exact same intervention to them that you did to your upper traps. Apply firm but not pain-inducing pressure to the trigger point for 20-30 seconds, then increase pressure to the next level of non-pain-inducing pressure. Do this for about 90 seconds total and you should feel the trigger point release.

The "stretch" after internal trigger point work can simply be deep, slow breathing, since the pelvic floor will descend and lengthen when you inhale. You could also increase this pelvic floor stretch by bringing yourself into child's pose.

Sit with your butt on your heels. This isn't possible for lots of people due to flexibility or knee issues but placing a pillow or blankets between your butt and your heels often helps. Please, for the love of all that is holy, do not sit in a W shape with your heels outside of your thighs (and if you see your child doing this, help them find a better sitting position). Place your hands on the ground in front of you and walk them out until you have stretched as far as you can comfortably reach. If flexibility prevents you from lying your arms flat on the ground with your forehead resting on the floor, use more pillows or blankets to support your top half.

Once you've achieved the position, breathe slowly and deeply, inviting yourself to relax further with each breath. Stay here as long as you'd like or until your feet fall asleep (another example of ischemic compression).

Use this technique to release trigger points but give the area a week of rest between sessions. You can perform this in any region of your body, and don't forget to perform stretching of the area afterward.

CHAPTER 7

PROLAPSE

As we defined earlier in the book, pelvic organ prolapse (POP) refers to the downward movement of organs within the pelvis. If your bladder protrudes into the vagina, this is called a cystocele. If the rectum protrudes into the vagina, this is called a rectocele. There are other forms of prolapse, which are all roughly named for what part of the body is protruding where.

POP is usually graded on a 0-4 scale (stage 0 is the least severe). One method is the POP-Q scale, which sounds like it's a compilation CD of the top 100 songs of today. But it's not that at all.

Stages of POP–Q system measurement[1]

Stage 0	no prolapse is demonstrated
Stage 1	the most distal portion of the prolapse is more than 1 cm above the level of the hymen
Stage 2	the most distal portion of the prolapse is 1 cm or less proximal or distal to the hymenal plane
Stage 3	the most distal portion of the prolapse protrudes more than 1 cm below the hymen but protrudes no farther than 2 cm less than the total vaginal length (for example., not all of the vagina has prolapsed)
Stage 4	vaginal eversion is essentially complete

Women who experience prolapse often report a sensation of heaviness, downward pressure, or fullness within their vagina. In a Stage 3 graded prolapse, women would feel something physically present in their vagina. In Stage 4, this would have prolapsed outside of their vagina and would be visible externally.

Remember the Boat Theory? If the pelvic floor muscles are not supporting the organs of the pelvis, then the ligaments supporting those organs are overstretched and the organs descend. We can improve support by improving awareness and function of the pelvic floor muscles. However, in the case of prolapse, there are overstretched ligaments. Ligaments are not well vascularized (meaning they don't have great blood flow), so they typically take longer to heal than skin or muscle injuries.

There is not great evidence on healing times for overstretched pelvic ligaments, but to use the medial collateral ligament (MCL) in the knee as an example, initial healing after injury can occur within two-three weeks, but further remodeling occurs over months and even years. The strength of the MCL can increase for up to 12 months post-injury, but after that it tapers off to only minimal increases.[2]

The problem with this is that POP isn't typically caused by an injury like an MCL sprain. It's often more of a slow building injury similar to what is often referred to as an "overuse" injury. I don't like that terminology because there's not a specific number of miles you can run before your knee gets an "overuse" injury. There's no certain number of jumping jacks you can do before your pelvic floor craps out. (Ask yourself if I said "craps out" on purpose.) However, faulty biomechanics (poor movements) over time will cause tissue irritation and eventually damage. You can "overuse" the heck out of something without ever having an injury if you're moving well. I digress.

If your pelvic ligaments are damaged over time and not immediately rehabilitated, we can assume that it will take longer than if there was a direct injury that you immediately began caring for. Since an injury like that requires at least a year to regain most strength, we can expect an even longer time for recovery. As such, the plan for rehabilitating pelvic organ prolapse is not a quick six-week fix. (Most things aren't.) We can certainly see improvements before six weeks but returning to full function (or as near to it as possible) will require significantly more time.

I say this while having a rather comprehensive Postpartum Rehabilitation program that is six weeks long.[3] Obviously the intention of that program is to rehabilitate postpartum (not just the pelvic floor, but the entire core; plus, it includes emotional healing techniques and postpartum education that seems to be missing from the general populace knowledge base). The reason why it's six weeks is because I couldn't get anyone to buy a two-year program. I'm kidding. Sort of. We can lay a foundation for healing and then continue to build upon that foundation. But building a foundation probably takes at least about six weeks.

Once you've established a foundation, you can build or revisit according to your needs. An example of this that is tangentially related to the pelvic floor is the formation of bunions (the bony growth outside of the big toe (or also pinky toe) with inward pointing of the big toe toward the rest of the toes). These can be construed as one of those "overuse injuries" that develop due to faulty biomechanics. Everyone thinks bunions are simply hereditary. There is evidence that some genetics play into their formation, but they're not entirely hereditary.[4]

Wolff's Law tells us that soft tissue dictates the formation of hard tissue. In other words, the forces of muscles and ligaments will determine how bone is formed.[5] The bony outgrowth of bunions is caused by the forces of the muscles of the foot pulling the big toe toward the other toes (and the low-level foot binding that we do by choosing shoes that compress our toes rather than allowing them to splay). This matters in relation to the pelvic floor (not just in the way that the foot bone's connected to the leg bone, the leg bone's connected to the thigh bone, etc.) because improving hip stabilization (which is done by the glute muscles of your pelvis) can help prevent hyperpronation (flattening) of the foot and bunion formation.[6]

I had the start of bunions at age 23. I was at my first-ever seminar on the gait cycle presented by the Motion Palpation Institute (shameless plug because I teach for them now and it's a great organization). I was one of the walkers who had my gait evaluated for a demonstration and the instructors pointed out the start of my big toes moving toward their smaller counterparts, and I was mortified. From that point forward, I put myself on a mission to change my foot function: I switched my daily shoes to ones that would let my toes move, eliminated high heels except for very special occasions, and worked intentionally on pelvic stability and foot awareness exercises.

I essentially stopped the bunions from worsening, but they weren't specifically improving. When I was 26, I discovered Correct Toes, which are toe spacers that help reshape your feet into a more neutral foot position. I wore them every single day for two years. (I told you I was a zealot.) This made a dramatic difference in my foot shape and the direction my big toes pointed. The extra bony growth didn't disappear, but my toes straightened out.

Now, ten years later, I wear Correct Toes sporadically and my toes are still pointing straight. Sometimes I will wear them a few times per week; sometimes I'll skip several weeks. I laid the foundation of solid foot function for several years, and now I can maintain that function without as much input. I took you on that little tangent to tell you that if you *actually* put in a solid foundation, you won't have to keep up with the same level of adherence forever. (I also told you that story so that you'd understand the importance of improving foot function as it relates to your pelvic floor.)

Pelvic rehabilitation can feel like a full-time job when you first start, and that can be really discouraging. But, just like a natural peanut butter or almond butter that comes with the oil separated on top of the solids, if you work really hard at the beginning, you can enjoy the fruits of your labor with minimal extra work later. (If you've never bought nut butter without stabilizers, you have no idea what I'm talking about; but if you know, you know.)

Regarding the importance of foot health in pelvic rehabilitation: one of the really cool things I learned from the DNS Women's Health course is the connection between a tall kneeling position (having an upright torso with one knee down and the opposite foot down on the ground) as the first time that the pelvis is uprighted in a normal developmental sequence in a baby.[7] This is simultaneously the first time that the baby's foot is fully flat and supporting the upright torso, as this movement happens before full standing or squatting. The connection between the foot and the pelvic floor therefore cannot be overstated.

If you're shod (which means to wear shoes and is a great word that's underutilized) all day every day, let those piggies wiggle free! One repeated measures study from 2015 found that people in athletic shoes had less balance than those going barefoot or wearing Vibram FiveFingers barefoot-style shoes.[8] It's worth getting more input from the world around you by letting your feet free.

Exercise - Bear Position

This exercise is one that I specifically give to my patients who are dealing with pelvic organ prolapse, but it's a great general exercise for improving pelvic floor stability without increasing load on your pelvic floor muscles. It's also great for strengthening the feet and toes, which you'll soon feel.

A 2021 study showed that this exercise specifically increased the tension of the abdominal wall, meaning it was one of the most effective exercises to elicit appropriate tension, not that the participants had inappropriate tension like the sucker-inners do.[9] This actually got better with cueing based on DNS principles, so we'll count this written description as a cue. We're going to revisit a movement milestone that you (hopefully) achieved at some point earlier in your life: bear position.

Around a year old, babies will beautifully lift their knees off the floor from a crawling position, using only their hands and toes for stability. This means they've got a lot of stabilization in their core because they don't have a lot of real estate keeping them stable on the ground (think of the difference between how stable you feel on tip toes vs. your full foot on the floor). But what's special about this position is that stability is achieved with the pelvic floor *above* the level of the diaphragm.

As we've discussed, having the diaphragm parallel to the pelvic floor allows us to adequately distribute IAP and maintain neutral posture. But maintaining this parallel position while simultaneously inverting it adds a little spice that many pelvic floors will enjoy. That was such a weird thing to write. Moving on.

Start on your hands and knees with your hands underneath your shoulders and your fingers fully splayed out and pressure evenly dispersed across all your big knuckles. Your knees should be slightly wider than your hips and your feet should be slightly narrower than your hips, but not touching. Tuck your toes underneath (so that the part of your toes that is normally on the ground is back on the ground), and lift from your butt to bring your knees up off the floor.

At this point, your diaphragm and pelvic floor are probably a smidge more parallel than they were before you lifted your knees because your arms are likely longer than your femurs. So now we need to get your diaphragm higher than your pelvic floor. Again, pulling from your glute (butt) muscles rather than pushing from your knees, lift your pelvis into the air. Your butt should be higher than your head, but your knees will stay bent so that you're not in a full downward dog yoga pose.

Keep the same hip hinging movement we've done before in mind as well as keeping your chin retracted so that you don't arch your back or have your head hanging below your chest.

Hang out here for one-three breaths, feeling expansion into your back and pelvis, and then slowly return to your hands and knees. Repeat the exercise at least five times, performing one-three breaths at the top of the bear position, then slowly returning to the ground.

As you become more comfortable in the position, you can increase the challenge by returning to the hovering position rather than returning to knees fully on the floor. You can also make things way harder by trying to pick up one hand or one foot off the floor without shifting your bodyweight. Don't try that until you've worked on the basics of this exercise three times per week for at least three weeks.

CHAPTER 8

SCAR TISSUE

Scar tissue indicates previous injury, and like all scars, they tell stories. Like Harry Potter's scar: that's an important scar. And just like Harry's scar, you ought to be able to feel your scars. Ideally not because a dark wizard is attempting to enter your mind - especially since we're talking about your pelvic floor - and my goodness, things certainly just got off track.

The points of the digression are that I like to relate things to Harry Potter whenever possible and that a significant issue of scars is that people don't think they're a problem if they can't feel them. But a lack of sensation is a big problem.

The pelvic floor is often covered, except (I've heard) in nudist colonies or in your own home. That means that there generally aren't a lot of ways that the pelvic floor can get scars from daily activities. But there are lots of scars in pelvic floors, especially in women.

If you give birth vaginally and you have a perineal or labial tear (which are graded based on their severity), you'll have scarring in that region. If you have an episiotomy cut during birth, you'll have a scar. If you give birth via cesar-ean section, you'll have an abdominal scar with internal scar tissue on your uterus. If you have a LEEP procedure, you'll have internal scar tissue on your cervix. If you have abdomi-nal surgery - yes, even laparoscopic* surgery - you'll have scars on your abdomen.

If you touch a scar and you can't feel it, that's not normal. It's called anesthesia, which translates to lack of sensation and is why anesthesia is called anesthesia. (Wow, what a line.)

- *Less* than normal sensation is called hypoesthesia.
- *More* than normal sensation is called hyperesthesia.
- *Weird* sensation is called paresthesia.

Paresthesia is sometimes experienced as a tingly sensation or the general sense of heebie-jeebies. Again, that's an official term. It has to be official because you just read it in a book from a doctor. Consider it doctrine.

A lot of people have abnormal sensation of scars and don't consider it to be a problem because it's not painful. Painful sensation is also abnormal, and the purpose of pain is

---

* I want to make a note on laparoscopic surgery in that it's seen as minimally invasive because of the scars themselves. It is outwardly minimally invasive but inwardly it can be even more invasive than a traditional cut. During laparoscopic surgery, the surgeons need to be able to see what they're working with, and as such, the abdomen is inflated to around the same size as a late second trimester or early third trimester pregnant abdomen. This inhibits the downward motion of the diaphragm and can impact the intra-abdominal pressure system after surgery, regardless of scars. Additionally, the pathway of the laparoscopic incisions essen-tially creates a tunnel of scar tissue internally that patients often report awareness of once we start working on their scars.

to indicate that we need to pay attention to the area. Think of pain like hyperesthesia - increased sensation.

The lack of appropriate sensation means that the brain is unable to perceive the region appropriately, which can (and does) lead to dysfunction of the area itself. In the next chapter, we'll discuss improving sensation in general. Please note: this is not a pass to skip ahead. Stick with me on this journey, young padawan.

Returning sensation to an area is more about brain perception than it is about the tissues involved. But the quality of the tissues themselves does impact how they respond. For this reason, if you are missing key nutrients in your diet, your soft tissues (skin, fascia, muscles, etc.) will show signs of deficiency and take longer to achieve normalcy. Conversely, in a randomized controlled trial, women who supplement with collagen peptides mixed with other nutrients demonstrate objective improvements in skin elasticity, hydration, and density. Their tissues responded favorably even one month following the cessation of the supplements.[1] In other words: our soft tissues fare better if we have the nutrients to support them.

Many of the anti-aging benefits touted by personal care products are based upon tissue health. The better hydrated and more mobile tissues are, the less wrinkled they look. But scars, unfortunately, don't tend to mobilize well.

Scars form cross-linked fibers when they heal. Scar tissue is thinner and more rigid than non-scarred tissue, and this is what makes them noticeable. The tissue that was damaged heals in a way that helps prevent re-injury to the area, but it's not quite the same as the tissue that it's replaced.

The brain knows about a scar because it was the driver behind the collagen fibrils connecting. There is also creation of blood vessels and nerve tissue in scars, meaning they're relatively normal from a nerve and blood supply perspective.[2] But proprioception (body awareness) and interoception (internal body sensation) is different in scar tissue because of how the brain perceives the area from before the scar was formed compared to after. The brain's "map" of what the area looks like is probably what it used to look like before the scar was there, so the scarred area doesn't match the map. A more severe version of this mismatch is phantom limb pain.

In phantom limb pain cases, people who have lost a limb experience pain in the limb that's missing. It's challenging because it's hard to treat an area that's not there, but this is a perfect example of how pain that we experience is actually felt in the brain and then mapped onto the body. Mirror therapy is often very beneficial for these patients because it helps the brain to re-map the area that it previously assigned to the limb to a different part of the body by the process of neuroplasticity (brain changing).

This brain re-mapping is what we need to do in scar tissues because the original tissue is no longer present, and the new tissue needs to be integrated into the brain appropriately.

To give a specific example of the case of a cesarean scar, most pregnant women experience some brain map changing because their abdomen expands in such a way that it's relatively unrecognizable from what it used to look like. The brain assimilates these changes (and I think it's part of the reason why pregnant women constantly rub their bellies - it gives them lots of sensory input about this new topography) over the course of pregnancy.

But in a cesarean surgery, the tissues are severed, and the blood and nerve supply have to re-grow. The brain's picture of what the abdomen looks like is now completely defunct: it's not the pre-pregnancy abdomen it had grown used to and it's also not the pregnant abdomen it had started to acknowledge. It's now got less sensory input and looks vastly different, so giving sensory input into this area through touch and soft tissue work helps prevent the brain from ignoring the area altogether.

For this reason, I like to work on scars - all of them - with patients and have some incredible results with very little input that you can achieve to some degree on your own.

Testimonial

I came in to see Dr. Mumma after a car accident. I had previously been under chiropractic care, so aside from some soreness after the wreck and a pre-existing foot injury, I had no general complaints. Upon the visit, she asked about my medical history, which she uncovered included three cesarean sections: 15, 12, and 8 years ago. In my third birth, I had an emergency partial hysterectomy (due to birthing complications). We were hoping for future pregnancies, so this changed our future of our family in an abrupt and painful way. It was extremely difficult to talk about my emergency partial hysterectomy and I knew I still had some emotional healing to do, but, 8 years later, I didn't consider that I still had physical healing to work on as well.

At my first visit, Dr. Mumma started working on my cesarean scar and I could immediately feel more sensation in it, which I had no idea was possible. I assumed after the emergency surgery I experienced that the nerve damage and numbness were permanent. I kept up with the exercises she gave me and did some scar tissue work at home as well. In my second visit with her, she did some more work on my scar. That evening, after the second visit, my husband gave me a hug and I just started crying. For the first time in 15 years, I could feel him hugging me right where the cesarean scar was located. It was an unbelievable feeling.

- Tara, 42

What I do with patients is exactly what I describe in the following exercise. I think there's a special element to having someone else care for a scar, and not just because it's hard to reach or because people train their hands and brains to palpate tissues and can be really good at it. I think it's more beneficial to work with someone - even if it's not a trained professional, but your friend or spouse or book club buddy who's also reading this book - because the element of re-learning the feel of the tissues can be easier if you aren't thinking of the process and are instead focused on the internal sensations (interoception).

I am cautious of overloading the brain with too much information at once. Scar tissue can quickly convert from hypoesthesia (too little sensation) to hyperesthesia (too much), so I try to take small steps rather than large leaps in returning sensation to an area. As you begin exploring your scars, be sure not to overwhelm your brain.

I also recommend that when you do scar tissue work, you don't take any mind- or state-altering substances that day. Don't map a new area of your body and then have a few cocktails, for example. I don't have a scientific study that points to why not, but I've found that the more a person can sink into feeling within their body without numbing or changing any of their sensations, the better their results seem to be.

Exercise - Scar Tissue Mobilization

I want you to start to feel your scars. If the way you got your scar is an emotionally-charged event, it might be particularly challenging for you to bring awareness to it. This can be very healing, but simultaneously challenging. Be aware of this and utilize whatever processing tools you've found beneficial if this applies to you: journaling, talking to a friend or loved one, meditation, counseling, going for a walk, diaphragmatic breathing with longer exhales and humming, etc. Regardless of if this is challenging, scars tend to bring up memories for people, so it might be a good idea to have a piece of paper to jot down any thoughts or reflections after you've completed this exercise.

If you have a scar in your abdomen or pelvic floor, choose that scar for this exercise. If not, pick any scar on your body because any amount of scar tissue can impact your whole body due to fascial connections.

If possible, expose the scar and look at it in a mirror so that you can see things from a different perspective, even if your scar is somewhere easily visible like your forearm. If it's internal or not able to be viewed, that's okay, but if you can see the scar at the same time that you touch the scar, your brain will get information from your eyes as well as your hands and can help normalize sensation.

Start by touching your scar and simply noticing how it feels both internally and to your hand. To the touch, scar tissue often feels smoother than skin and more slippery if it's located in a mucous membrane (for example: vagina, perineum, or mouth); it typically feels denser when it's on external skin. Internally, it likely will have a slightly different sensation than your other tissues - hyper-, hypo-, or paresthesia. If you can look in the mirror, watch yourself touching the scar to help your brain perceive it normally.

If your scar is anywhere on your torso, breathe into the scar. If your scar is somewhere else, close your eyes and envision your breath expanding to the scar. Don't force it, just allow the scar to expand on inhale and relax on exhale. Feel the expansion with your hand and note any changes in internal sensation. Repeat for 5-10 breaths.

If your scar holds particular grief and this was emotionally challenging for you, stop there and return to this exercise tomorrow or the next day. Move on to the next part when doing the exercise as described thus far is no longer emotionally challenging.

Now slowly run your finger back and forth over the scar in several directions with non-painful pressure from your finger(s) and note if you can pick up on any tugging or pulling sensation indicating that the scar is tethered to other tissues. If you find that moving the scar in one direction produces a catching, pulling, or tugging sensation (either internally or externally), you're going to mobilize it. If you don't *feel* a difference but can *see* the scar and the tissues around it move easily in one direction, and not as easily in another direction, you'll mobilize it toward the area it isn't moving.

With your finger pads (not tips) placed as close to the scar as possible but not directly on the scar, pull slightly in the direction you feel or see resistance. I teach my patients (as well as the students and doctors in my continuing ed classes) that I want them to *invite* the scar to move toward them. This should be a gentle mobilization and not a stretch or painful pull. Then apply a little bit more non-painful pressure downward into whatever tissue is below your finger pads. With this slight increase in pressure and still pulling in the direction of the restriction, move perpendicular to the direction of resistance, back and forth.

If you're palpating internal tissue, not looking in a mirror, or otherwise completely confused right now, just pull a bit on the scar while pressing slightly and move your finger around a bit.

You can progress this exercise by gently pinching and rolling the scar and underlying tissues. You can then use two hands or two fingers moving in opposing directions to work perpendicular to the direction of the scar. If the scar is on the outside of your body, you can utilize cupping (which is definitely better when done by a professional but can be accomplished on your own) or even percussion (think massage guns, but one that ideally oscillates at a rate of 50-60 cycles per second), which has been shown to temporarily relax a muscle and improve circulation.[3]

Revisit this exercise as often as you are able. If there's no particular emotional response, it's a great idea to work on scars for five minutes or so at least twice a week until sensation feels relatively normal. Revisit any scars about once every six-eight weeks to make sure sensation stays adequate.

CHAPTER 9

LACK OF AWARENESS

Lack of awareness affects lots of areas of your body. In a backwards sort of way, we've already addressed a lot of this in earlier chapters, but I wanted to delineate this specifically within its own chapter because awareness is so important, and it's also its own issue. It is both a form of hypoesthesia *and* a decreased proprioception. Remember: awareness brings choice. Choice is better than no choice.

You probably felt an increase in awareness of your pelvic floor when we first did the exercise of palpating your perineum while breathing. This increase in awareness helped you find your breath descending into your pelvic floor, which helped to improve your breathing pattern.

You likely increased awareness of your breath simply by beginning to pay attention to how you are doing something that you've been doing without awareness since you first entered the world. You also increased your spatial awareness of the posture of your head, neck, feet, and even your tongue with earlier exercises.

Increasing awareness of your posture, breath, and body is an endeavor of its own that is worth undertaking simply for the sake of more intentionally inhabiting your soul's container. Is that too dramatic? (I told you I missed the opportunity to double for Brooke Shields.) Living with more awareness can help you be more mindful rather than mindless. It can help you improve your ability to perceive different levels of sensation.

My friend and family doctor, Dr. Elizabeth Sierakowski, reminds me of this fact when I need to hear it: *you are a human being, not a human doing.* It can be hard to just *be*, but when we stop doing, we can usually sink into better awareness (and also often acceptance). This comes in quite handy during labor (though I didn't meet her until I was done having kids, so that was sort of inconvenient for me personally).

I teach a very basic childbirth education class and have had many birthing women report that identifying the sensations they felt during labor helped them significantly decrease their perception of pain.[1] Remember from our discussion of the Polyvagal Theory that perception is an incredibly important part of how you experience your surroundings. If you experience pain and that scares you, you will likely tense up as a result, which can actually increase pain.

Dr. Grantly Dick-Read, a British obstetrician in the early 20th century who wrote the book *Natural Childbirth* amidst the ongoing trend of twilight sleep (both analgesia and amnesia during birth), called this the Fear-Tension-Pain

(FTP) cycle.[2] He advocated for reducing fear through education about what's normal in childbirth and encouraging relaxation, both of which would disrupt this cycle. Most childbirth education classes have stemmed from his ideas, including mine.

But beyond the FTP cycle, there's also the delineation of a painful sensation in general. If a woman is more acutely aware of an increase in pressure rather than attributing any new sensation in labor as "painful," this is incredibly helpful in increasing comfort. Her body can perceive the difference between pulling, pressure, heaviness, tightness, stretching, constriction, cramping, or burning. All of those are sensations commonly experienced during labor.

If we had a limited number of sensations to choose from and had to operate from general categories such as Painful, Pleasurable, or Inconsequential, then most of those sensations would fall under the heading of Painful. But by delineating further, we get more nuance and detail, which ideally helps us create clarity around our current state of being and feeling.

The same is true outside of labor, of course. Another example is experiencing our cold tub. We have a Plunge at my office. It is delightful: 39 degrees of circulating cold water in a pristine white tub of glory. Some people disagree about the "glory" part, but the rest is a factual description. We use it for injury rehab, sports recovery, swelling reduction, decreasing inflammation, and overall mental and emotional wellbeing.

Cryotherapy (cold therapy) has also been shown to be beneficial for postpartum perineal pain.[3] After lochia (pronounced LO-kia, which is postpartum bleeding, not a Norse god) has passed (between two and eight weeks postpartum), we encourage women to experience the Plunge.

While everyone who enters the Plunge has a different mental and emotional response to the water, the expected response of their physical sensation is cold, burning, aching, and numbness.[4] When I guide patients through the experience, I let them know this order of sensations ahead of time. I then encourage them to try to identify those sensations specifically rather than solely the initial response of shock, panic, and concern about getting into cold water that (upon extended exposure) could actually cause hypothermia or eventually death. This often helps them relax in the tub more, even though the water is still quite frigid.

It's easy to recognize the importance of this level of nuance in relation to art. My Back Office Manager (we call her the BOM), Mary (when talking about planning her wedding and picking colors with her fiancé) said that Van Gogh didn't go to a paint store and just ask for "blue." Think of Van Gogh's level of blue delineation and apply that to your own level of body sensation. The more specific you can get, the more beautiful the picture you're painting for yourself of your internal experience.*

The same is true for your emotional sensations. Dr. Gloria Wilcox created the Feelings Wheel, which helps people identify exactly what they're feeling, rather than just broad

---

* I left this paragraph untouched. I wrote it several weeks before Mary was killed and am grateful to see her memorialized in this very normal way in print.

generalizations of Mad, Scared, Joyful, Powerful, Peaceful, or Sad. Each of those six feelings is broken down into six more specific feelings, and then those feelings are broken down into two more feelings: one filled in and one blank space to be filled in by the participant as appropriate.[5]

We differentiate types of sensation in patient examinations because it helps to give us as practitioners an idea of the health of the patient's nervous system communication. We test a person's perception to light and sharp sensations and two-point discrimination because this can let us know about the communication between the body and the brain and vice versa. We can also do some general proprioceptive tests to determine a patient's balance and their response to their environment.

A fun test to do is one on a person's general proprioceptive acuity. I learned this from a mentor years ago and don't have a study to point to, but feel free to recreate the exercise yourself. I have a patient stand beside a white board (or piece of paper taped to the wall) where I've drawn a dot. I give the patient a marker, have them stand perpendicular to the wall and let them look at where the dot is before closing their eyes and facing forward. With their eyes closed and their entire body facing perpendicular to the white board, I ask them to make a mark as close to the original dot as possible. With their eyes still closed, they return their arm to their side, and then repeat the attempt two more times.

Patients who are in pain tend to perform poorly. Their dots are all over the board. After I adjust them, we repeat the test. This is by no means a scientific study, but every single patient I've ever done this with showed marked improvement in their dot test (as in their three dots were closer to the original than in their pre-adjustment test).

I've waited nine chapters to tell you about how great chiropractic care is. I've only briefly mentioned it thus far. I did that for several reasons. The first is because I want you to understand your pelvic floor and what might be problematic about it, and I want you to learn how your whole body and lifestyle impact your pelvic floor. Then I want you to get the absolute best results by putting all of this together, which ideally includes the secret sauce to this recipe we're concocting throughout this book: chiropractic care.

The most basic way of describing to you what it is that I do as a chiropractor is that I examine the body through active and passive movement, palpation, observation, and testing to discover areas that move well (and leave them alone), move too much (and give exercises and feedback to help stabilize them), or move too little (and apply adjustments, mobilizations, and exercises to help mobilize them).

A chiropractic adjustment merely introduces motion into a joint that is moving poorly. Sometimes this produces a cracking or popping sound that was previously called a cavitation (collapse of gas bubbles) but is more recently being referred to as a tribonucleation (cavity formation).[6] We aren't putting bones back into place; we're introducing motion into joints.

Just like with aberrant (not normal) sensation of the body, you can have aberrant movement of the body: too much, too little, or just weird. Chiropractors can normalize movement with adjustments. Some really cool studies have been done that show that adjustments can actually increase a person's general proprioception.[7] This is why people improve in the dot test after chiropractic care.

Chiropractic adjustments can actually improve brain function by decreasing cerebellar inhibition.[8] Both of those studies I just referenced were done on people with sub-clinical neck pain, meaning they weren't actively in pain at the time, but showed signs of joint dysfunction that chiropractors addressed via adjustments. This is important because most people associate chiropractic care with pain relief, but these two studies just showed us that pain isn't a necessary component of improving function with chiropractic care.

Dr. Heidi Haavik was part of both of those studies, and she was also part of the study that showed us how impactful chiropractic care is specifically on the pelvic floor of pregnant women. In a study she conducted, women in their second trimester of pregnancy received a chiropractic adjustment and demonstrated an increased levator hiatal (opening) area at rest.[9] This means that their pelvic floor relaxed after an adjustment to their spine. This did not happen in the control (non-pregnant) group, meaning that it was a pregnancy-related effect.

Can you perceive how relaxation of the pelvic floor during pregnancy would be important? For a baby to pass through the birth canal (which is also known as your vagina), the pelvic floor muscles will need to lengthen and allow for expansion.

I view this post-adjustment relaxation like Braxton Hicks contractions. A lot of midwives I know call Braxton Hicks "practice contractions" because they are the same uterine contractions that will guide baby through the birthing process, but because they lack the hormonal cascade of labor, they're not productive other than practicing repetitions. These reps can potentially help to tone the uterus.

The uterus comprises smooth muscle, just like your heart and lungs. One of the many benefits of working out is that it strengthens your heart and lungs through repetitions of these smooth muscles contracting, and this is what many think Braxton Hicks are doing: strengthening the uterus through repetitive contractions.

We have evidence to support that women who see a chiropractor during their first pregnancy have approximately 25% shorter labor times compared to women who don't see a chiropractor. Subsequent pregnancies see labor times shorten by approximately 31%.[10] I have several theories on this, but we don't have an exactly clear picture as to why labor is shorter in women who've seen a chiropractor. Since this book is about the pelvic floor and not about pregnancy, I'll keep my theories short: I think part of it stems from the pelvic floor relaxation that occurs after an adjustment - it's sort of like a "practice relaxation" instead of a "practice contraction."

I can't imagine going through pregnancy without chiropractic care, personally. I also really can't imagine going through life without chiropractic care. I've seen a chiropractor since I was 15. I had SI joint pain for a year that no one could help me with, and no imaging or tests could uncover a reason for. Most providers told me I was too young for back pain. I agreed with them, but I still had back pain. My chiropractor was the first person who said she could help me, and she did. I've only had one other instance of SI pain since then, and that was during my second pregnancy when a hemorrhoid thrombosed (read: pelvic pain as a result of pelvic floor dysfunction).

Chiropractic care itself can be beneficial for improving continence in patients. A case series of 13 elderly patients receiving adjustment only (no additional therapy or exercises) for one-eight weeks, showed participants' bladder control (measured as nighttime waking to urinate (nocturia), urgency, leakage, and pad changes) improved significantly.[11]

The benefits of chiropractic care are numerous and include improvements in pelvic floor function. If you're not already a chiropractic patient, I hope I've convinced you of its necessity, regardless of whether or not you have symptoms. If you're already a chiropractic patient, be sure to include your chiropractor in your plans for improving your pelvic floor (and gift them a copy of this book).

Exercise - Full Body Awareness

If you want to know what's in my head while I write this exercise out for you, look up Bastille's song "Laura Palmer."[12] (The chorus is what I'm singing.)

This exercise has two parts (three if you count looking up the song). For the first part, I want you to stand with your feet flat on the ground. Starting at your head, you're going to touch your whole body. Place both of your palms onto your head and gently but firmly press your hands down (as if your hands were hugging you) for about a second, and then move them to another part of your head. Attempt to cover every inch of you with touch.

Go from your head to your face to your neck to your left arm, then your right arm, then your chest and as much of your back as you can touch, then your abdomen, then your pelvis and gooch/taint/perineum, then your butt, then your left leg, then your right leg, and then both feet. You get it: touch your whole self.

Now you've got a little bit of increased awareness of your body. The second part of the exercise is to exist with this extra awareness intentionally. Perhaps you stand and feel, breathing in and out with your eyes closed and feeling what your sense of *self* now is. Maybe you lie down and experience the increased sensation while resting into that human *being* idea.

Pay attention to the sensations. Consider if you feel pulsing, pressure, heaviness, lightness, expansiveness. Can you feel your breath expanding into more places on your torso? Can you feel your pulse drumming throughout your body?

Can you hear me singing that Bastille song?

This is your heart: can you feel it, can you feel it? Pumps through your veins, can you feel it, can you feel it?

That's what I'm hoping for you. I want you to feel your heart pumping blood through your body. I hope that's not gross sounding if you're squeamish. I am not a squeamish person, so I apologize if I just ruined the book for you. Moving on.

This is a great pre-shower exercise. If you take warm showers and wait for the water to warm up, a quick version of this exercise takes about the amount of time to go through as your hot water tank takes to heat up your shower. If you enjoy the benefits of cold showers like I do, I still sometimes wait outside the shower while I hype myself up to step into the cold water. But this is also a great exercise to do while in the shower, regardless of if it's hot or cold. Try adding this before/during your shower at least once per week and maybe try out the option where you lie down and drift into a meditation with this heightened sense of interoception.

PART 3

COMMON PFD
INTERVENTIONS

CHAPTER 10

EVIDENCE-INFORMED CARE

I'm going to give you my evidence-informed approach here. That's what I've been doing all along, but this is the part of the book where some people are going to start to get a little frustrated with me - especially if they're pelvic health professionals - because I am going to say things that contradict what they are saying/doing.

Health professionals generally like to do things the way that they do them. They find or are taught a way to do XYZ and have some success with patients, so they continue doing it that way and assume it's the "right" or "best" way to do XYZ (or sometimes they have no success but still dig their heels in). Discovering that you're doing something to or with a patient that is not productive at best or counterproductive at worst is a hard pill to swallow. And we'll often point to our success cases to argue that the things we're doing *are* working. But sometimes successes happen despite our treatments.

I used to do a really deep mobilization for the posterior shoulder capsule (back part of the shoulder joint) in patients who'd had a specific shoulder injury or dysfunction. Once they could reach a certain level of flexibility, I viewed the treatment as a success. The patient often felt better as well. Then I went to a throwing seminar and learned that the posterior shoulder capsule was usually tight because of instability and was tight as a protection for the patient rather than as a problem.

I had a light bulb moment and switched to checking shoulder stability in some new ways and discovered that those patients with whom I'd done aggressive stretching were really unstable and at huge risk of future injury - especially if they were overhead athletes. I had to backtrack with those patients and give them new exercises and metrics.

It kind of sucked to have to do that, but those patients all appreciated that I'd learned something new and was willing to share it rather than continuing them on a path that was potentially going to end up with them having a worse shoulder injury.

That was an instance where the symptom wasn't a problem but was a signal of something else that was happening that needed to be addressed. It's like taking a Tylenol for a broken arm. Sure, the pain has diminished, but the problem is still present.

And that segues into another example that I want to share with you regarding evidence-based care. Please note that I told you I'd be providing you with my evidence-*informed* approach and now I'm talking about evidence-*based* approaches. Evidence-based practitioners are quite proud of their willingness and ability to perform treatments that are soundly based in scientific findings that can be duplicated in research. These are great practices and it's a wonderful idea to perform only evidence-based treatments.

But.

Researchers in manual therapy study treatments that are being done already. Sure, sometimes someone comes up with a brand-new tool or technique and will test it out in a trial first. But most of the time, they're investigating what's already being done in practice. I've seen estimates of 10-20 years of lag time between when a treatment is backed by evidence and when it trickles its way into regular practice. Meanwhile, we have patients to see, problems to solve, and people to help.

What I'm saying is that sometimes we have to bridge the gap between what we know to be the best evidence available and where we currently are with a patient. Chiropractic care is best paired with exercise, according to lots of research. But some patients don't do their exercises. I don't refuse to treat these patients because they're not following an evidence-based model of care. I simply encourage them to participate in their healthcare and remind them how helpful their exercises are.

Another example is an anti-inflammatory diet. There is a ton of evidence that patients who are not eating processed foods have better health markers than those who are. Most of my patients hear about an anti-inflammatory diet, but I'm not going to wait to treat them until they've cleaned up their pantry and refrigerator. I'm going to meet them where they are, suggest small changes, and give them the best care I can.

The evidence shows that they would recover from whatever ails them faster if they weren't eating processed foods, but I'm going to offer them the best care regardless.

Dr. Karel Lewit was an incredible doctor and professor and founded the Prague School of Manual Medicine and Rehabilitation. I considered him a mentor even though I never got to meet him before his passing. He is quoted as saying, "We work at the acceptable level of uncertainty," regarding evidence-based medicine.[1]

We won't and can't know everything. But we can work at that acceptable level of uncertainty and help patients along the way. This is my approach: ensure that what I'm doing is based on sound clinical reasoning, is acceptable to the patient, and relies on available clinical research whenever possible. That doesn't mean that everything I do in practice has a research article behind it. It also doesn't mean I'll do something just because the mood strikes me. I'm bridging the gap between evidence that's available and what the patient and I determine to be their best course of care.

In quick succession, I'll let you know some of the evidence we have for pelvic floor therapies and treatments, but I am by no means addressing all of the millions of articles present on PubMed. I did not comb all of the available evidence because I have a husband, children, a business, and hobbies. What I do in general is search the Cochrane Library and PubMed for Randomized Controlled Trials (RCT) or Systematic Reviews regarding common interventions for PFD. When those aren't available, I look to lower quality studies. Then I see if it matches up with what I'm practicing and what my patients value or are willing to do.

I have investigated a variety of interventions for PFD and want to share with you some snippets of what I've uncovered. As stated, this is not an exhaustive list, but I selected some examples of studies that show a variety of information to give you a bit of an overview. Here goes.

We have decent evidence that pelvic floor muscle training and lifestyle changes can improve symptoms of pelvic floor dysfunction, including pelvic organ prolapse (POP) and incontinence.[2] The evidence is promising more than conclusive, but it exists.[3] Pessaries tend to come with side effects and minimal supportive evidence (more on those in a bit).[4] Pelvic floor muscle training has been found to be superior to hypopressive (negative pressure) exercises for treating pelvic organ prolapse.[5] There is limited evidence for the use of estrogen for the treatment of POP, though it is frequently recommended alongside pessary use.[6] Pelvic floor muscle training has been shown to be effective for diminishing dyspareunia.[7]

A pessary is a device that is fitted by a gynecologist or urogynecologist to be inserted into the vagina. It is often the first treatment recommended for pelvic organ prolapse and recommended as a treatment for stress urinary incontinence. They can cause side effects such as vaginal bleeding and discharge, increased incontinence, or irritation of the vaginal wall.[4]

Some doctors recommend the use of a tampon to serve the same purpose of offering physical support to the vaginal wall to help eliminate the symptoms of a cystocele (bladder prolapse). I feel fairly certain that no woman has ever recommended that another woman stick a tampon into her non-bleeding vagina because it is a most unpleasant feeling to pull a dry tampon from one's vagina. I know many of you cringed upon reading that, but that's my point: it's a cringe-worthy suggestion.

Regarding tampons in general, these findings were not statistically significant, but tampon users showed higher mercury levels and oxidative stress biomarkers than non-tampon users.[8] So in addition to being a generally crappy recommendation to shove something into your vagina to prevent an organ from pushing into it, this recommendation also comes with risk of extra exposure of some of your most delicate tissues to nasty ingredients. For the record, I think menstrual cups were a great invention (these are not new and were originally patented in the 1800s as catamenial sacks).[9]

General Recommendations

If I were to ask anyone what general recommendation they'd have for a pelvic floor exercise, they would almost certainly say "kegel." Would they know that Arnold Kegel was a doctor and his three-step approach to studying and working with the pelvic floor involved a observation, palpation, and then insertion of a manometer or perineometer that measured the contractile strength of the pelvic floor?[10] Or would they think that they're just supposed to squeeze their pelvic floor at every red light (or pretend to start and stop the flow of urine) for the rest of their lives?

Because, as you've no doubt surmised, Dr. Arnold Kegel *was* a gynecologist, and he didn't just tell people to squeeze their nether regions. He *observed* weakness in the levator ani group muscles of his patients, *palpated* their pelvic floor musculature, and then *inserted* a device to offer feedback to patients on how strongly they were contracting their pelvic floor muscles. His work has been bastardized to a simple suck and squeeze maneuver that women are hand waved toward.

A lot of practitioners and social media influencers have convinced people that they just aren't doing their kegels correctly, and also often add that doing them incorrectly will cause more problems. If you have POP and kegel incorrectly, you could in theory make things worse by increasing downward pressure on an already injured pelvic floor. But in general, squeezing some muscles in your own body is not a cause of concern. Humans have strong self-preservation traits, so it's unlikely that we'd continue an exercise to our own irreversible detriment.

But that's not what I have a problem with. The problem isn't that people aren't kegeling correctly, it's that they think that kegels will save their pelvic floor. There's an assumption of pelvic floor weakness as the prime driver of all pelvic floor dysfunction that kegel exercises would improve via contraction.

We simply don't have strong enough evidence that women have perpetually weak pelvic floors. If they did, then it's possible that concentric contraction (shortening) of your pelvic floor muscles would help. But that wouldn't improve a hypertonic (too tense) pelvic floor, would it? Could that be why everyone seems to know what a kegel is and we still have a significant number of women who are peeing their pants?

Pelvic floor hypertonicity is often a learned behavior of holding the pelvic floor tight.[11] Some people might've started holding their pelvic floor tight in an effort to avoid incontinence, and then had increased incontinence as a result of holding their pelvic floor tight. Maybe you're one of them. That learned behavior of holding tension in your pelvic floor isn't going to get better by you squeezing your vagina. That would be like me telling you to get your traps to relax by repetitively shrugging your shoulders (kind of like how you used to when chest breathing, which you of course haven't done since before reading Chapter 2). Though it might be beneficial for you to shrug your shoulders up as high as possible once or twice just so that you could feel how incredible it feels to relax them fully afterward. The same can be done with a pelvic floor contraction, but that's clearly not the same as repetitively kegeling.

Other women have pelvic floor hypertonicity due to an injury from pelvic surgery. Others can experience this due to acute or chronic pain in the pelvis.[11]

Many issues within the pelvic floor will have the response of increasing tension within the pelvic floor. This is the body's typical response to injury: hold it tight until we know for sure it's safe to move. It's what you do if you step off a curb and twist your ankle or if you fall on your arm and hurt it. This works for short-term protection but not for long-term function. Remember: holding tension is how we form trigger points.

One study that Dr. Paul Hodges (more on him in a bit) was part of showed that women who had SUI (stress urinary incontinence) had decreased balance compared to women who were continent.[12] The conclusion of that study specifically stated: "Increased activity of the PF and trunk muscles in women with SUI may impair balance as a result of a reduced contribution of trunk movement to postural correction or compromised proprioceptive acuity."

To translate that for you, if the pelvic floor and trunk are *hypertonic* (too tight), the body can't move as well and doesn't have as much spatial awareness, which could increase the risk of falls.

Considering that nursing homes are full of people who are there due to incontinence, and the terrifying reality of falls in elderly patients, incontinence certainly is something that no amount of hand waving will make me ignore.

On a relatively related note, eight weeks of diaphragmatic breath training (just like you're practicing) resulted in improved balance in healthy individuals.[13] It seems to me like if you improve both ends of the abdominal canister - the diaphragm and the pelvic floor - you'd be pretty well-balanced, eh?

I think I've made the case thus far that a lot of different factors can affect your pelvic floor health. If you rely on one exercise to "fix" a multifactorial issue, you'll fall short.

If you've ever been taught how to deadlift, your coach didn't tell you how to individually contract your hamstring muscles as part of the instruction. If they did, that was weird. They probably demonstrated how to deadlift, then instructed you on *movements* rather than muscle contractions. The purpose of a deadlift is to be able to pick things up off the ground, and you can improve your overall strength if you train this movement (which I recommend you do).

The purpose of doing a kegel is (drumroll, please) to kegel. There's not an event wherein you'd need to squeeze and lift your pelvic floor in isolation. Having the ability to suck your pelvic floor up to your eyeballs is only helpful for completing the activity of sucking your pelvic floor up to your eyeballs. There is no translatable skill that you'll garner from kegeling. Sure, you might need to contract your pelvic floor while rushing to the bathroom - especially if you're experiencing incontinence already - but when you hold a kegel and then try to do anything else, you've put a dent in that abdominal canister. That's a short-term strategy that isn't a long-term functional movement.

I don't tell my patient's to kegel. They're using their pelvic floor muscles already, so if I can help them get awareness of their full body - breath, posture, jaw, feet, pelvis - we can usually improve their ability to use these muscles more efficiently. If, instead, we break down the individual components of how the pelvic floor muscles contract, we likely won't have as great of success.

What you need is a pelvic floor that responds to your environment - internally and externally. If you sneeze, your pelvic floor needs to withstand the massive and rapid increase in intra-abdominal pressure that is exerted downward. If you need to walk across the room, your pelvic floor needs to help stabilize your torso when you take a step. Walking across the room requires each side of your pelvic floor to respond differently. If you kegel, you interrupt this appropriate asymmetrical pelvic floor activity.

Because your pelvic floor does more than simply contract for pelvic floor exercises, I argue that a deadlift (especially a single leg deadlift) would be a much better pelvic floor training strategy than a kegel. The pelvic floor is an integral part of the dynamics of a deadlift - along with the hamstrings, glutes, and core. And like any other muscle group, we need to be able to relax those muscles before activating. If you try to deadlift or squat while squeezing your butt muscles, it won't work well. You have to allow the glutes to lengthen and relax before activating. Squeezing/shortening them concentrically just isn't the same as activating through movement.

Dr. Paul Hodges, whom I just mentioned, has a doctorate in physiotherapy and two in neuroscience, and has contributed significantly to the world of manual therapy via research. He has published several studies on the role of the pelvic floor and abdominal wall. According to his biography at the University of Queensland, continence is one of five areas of research interest. He's published A LOT of work over the years, and because of that, he's well known within rehab circles.

Just to give you a taste of some of what he's contributed just specifically related to the pelvic floor: in one study from 2007, he showed how the pelvic floor had a role in both postural and respiratory functions, and had an anticipatory role in creating spinal stiffness (meaning the pelvic floor would preemptively help keep the spine stable).[14] In 2014, he was part of a study that demonstrated a relationship between low back pain, incontinence, breathing disorders, and gastrointestinal symptoms.[15] The authors found that the presence of one of those symptoms increased the risk of developing another one of those symptoms. He had been part of a study in 2009 that specifically showed that any of the aforementioned increased the risk of back pain, so demonstrating that the reverse was also true was a new and important finding.[16]

But one of Hodges' studies seemed to have a greater impact than others. Hodges published extensively on the importance of the role of the transversus abdominis (TrA) in trunk stability. Similar to his 2007 study that I referenced above wherein he (and other researchers, but I tend to focus on Hodges because his work is familiar to me; by no means do I mean to disrespect his co-authors by failing to mention them) showed that the pelvic floor had an anticipatory role in stability, he showed in 1999 that the TrA fired preemptively in healthy individuals before movement. He also found that people who had low back pain did not fire their TrA first, as is appropriate.[17] That was the end of the study.

We (meaning manual therapists and fitness professionals in general) extrapolated from that study that we needed to engage the TrA and to do so *yesterday*. This is what I learned in chiropractic college, and then heard in fitness classes and yoga classes and from the interwebs at large. The easiest way to contract the transversus abdominis is by pulling the belly button toward the spine. Now you know why everyone tells you to pull your belly button to your spine, even though it's a bass-ackward approach to stabilizing your torso (as I hope you've gathered by this point in the book).

You can see how this response was repeated: *this study shows us that this muscle group doesn't activate when things aren't going well, so the natural solution is to suck that muscle group in and that will solve all of our problems.*

Hodges also showed in 2007 how the pelvic floor muscles were delayed in activating in women who had incontinence compared to those who didn't, and this worsened as their bladder filled.[18] And in another study from 2007, Hodges showed that women who experienced incontinence had *increased* pelvic floor and abdominal muscle activity, which again challenged the assumption that these muscles had reduced activity (were simply weak) in those experiencing incontinence.[19]

In yet another 2007 Hodges study (it was a busy year), he showed that feedforward contraction (pre-emptive, anticipatory loading) of the TrA was not influenced by the direction of arm movement, meaning that bilateral activation of the TrA would create better stability, regardless of what the body was doing.[20] But in 2008, two other researchers from another Australian university (Drs. Sue Morris and Garry Allison from Curtin University) printed the first study that showed that feedforward activation of the TrA was *specific* to the direction arm movement, and therefore the idea of sucking in the TrA bilaterally was completely backward.[21] This was clearly the opposite finding of Hodges' study.

Morris and Allison published more research, as researchers do, and doubled down in a 2012 study showing that training TrA to activate prior to exertion to avoid low back pain was faulty.[22] That study demonstrated that the whole body worked synergistically.

Morris and Allison further published a rebuttal to the corset hypothesis (sucking in to stabilize) and in their conclusion stated: "These findings indicate that training bilateral pre-activation of the transversus abdominis prior to rapid movement is not justified and may potentially be problematic for the production of normal movement patterns."[23]

The final study I want to share is a 2015 study done by Mota et al. showed that the inter-rectus distance (the space between the two six-pack muscles in the front of your abdomen) actually *increased* when participants were cued to suck in.[24] That study is specific to treatment of a diastasis (which we'll briefly talk about in the next chapter), but it's indicative of the core not functioning optimally. If a method creates a greater dent or leak in your abdominal canister, so to speak, it isn't one I'm going to lean heavily on.

I share all of this research to show you a few things:

1. Why practitioners disagree on the best approaches to care.

2. How much evidence exists for and against specific ideas.

3. How different researchers can find different results from nearly identical studies.

4. How interpretation of these studies in clinical practice can significantly impact outcomes.

So where do we land after all of that? I've only selected a few handfuls of research, and there is plenty more out there. Here's what I take away: the pelvic floor and core function together. When one aspect of that synergistic system is malfunctioning, the whole thing malfunctions. We consistently find that the whole body responds to various stimuli, and in healthy individuals, we see that things proactively fire, though our ability to recreate that within a dysfunctional or painful system is lacking. We also have seen that pelvic floors can malfunction when they are tight rather than weak, and this can lead to decreased balance as well as further dysfunction.

To bring that summation into clinical practice, I remove the suck in/pull in method of core activation (meaning of the TrA and the pelvic floor as in a kegel) and instead focus on the whole body's ability to respond to its environment by improving awareness of body posture and loading. I imagine that reading through some of those studies was confusing, as many of them are contradictory, but I'm hoping that as you continue using your core and pelvic floor differently through the exercises in this book, you'll find more clarity.

Exercise - Functional Progression 2

The Functional Progression was created by Dr. Erica Boland using the principles of DNS. This is part two of a four-part movement sequence (you can find the rest on her practice YouTube channel, Coulee Health) that essentially mimics a human's first year of life from a movement developmental standpoint. This exercise starts with the basics of a low oblique sit, which happens around seven months old, and adds in some specific pelvic floor activity along with abdominal wall activation, hip mobility and stability, and shoulder stability. It's a lot of bang for your buck.

Begin lying on your right side, propped up on your right elbow with your right hand flat on the ground and your hips and knees bent. If you have a protractor handy, your hips should be bent so that your femur is about 120 degrees from your torso and your knees are bent to 90 degrees. I am obviously kidding about the protractor, but you want your knees to be bent so that they're in front of the plane of your torso, meaning your heels will be in line with your hips, which are stacked on top of each other. Your heels, hips, shoulders, and ears ought to be in one straight line.

Depending on when you graduated high school, you might have a senior picture in this pose.

We want to take this from sultry senior portrait to active core and pelvic floor stability work, so lift the left side of your torso toward the ceiling until you're no longer slouching into your right side, but your ribs are in line with your pelvis.

Press the outside of your right knee into the ground so that you can elevate your right hip at the same time that you bring both hips forward until you end with your knees, hips, and shoulders in one line and your feet behind the plane of your body. Then, using the hip hinge movement we've already practiced, hinge back down to the starting position.

For your next rep, add movement of the top (left) leg by rotating your left femur so that your knee faces toward the ceiling while you slowly kick the inside of your left foot toward the midline of your body. Get your right hip to fully extend like it did on the last rep, and then bring both hips back and down to the starting position. You might look like you're trying to kick a hacky sack to the casual observer, though I doubt you'd be very successful in this horizontal position. Do five total reps and then repeat on your left side.

This exercise can be complicated but is wonderful for pelvic floor activity that isn't sucking in and uses both sides of the pelvic floor in different ways. It also works the glutes quite nicely and creates a cross-body activation of the core. Avoid overarching your back and make sure that your rib cage isn't flared up (sticking out) when you perform this. It's also important to note that you don't try to suck in or kegel while doing this exercise because that would be counterproductive.

Try adding this three times per week with at least five reps on each side.

CHAPTER 11

CONTRACT ON EXERTION (AND WHY I DON'T RECOMMEND IT)

Every. Single. Program. I am constantly being asked by patients, students, and readers alike if _____ is a good program for pelvic floor rehabilitation. The answer is almost always no. And it's not for lack of trying. People put together great programs with excellent graphics, images, audio, flow, and video. But they're based on incomplete or inaccurate information. Regardless of format, the program sucks if the content sucks. And if the content tells you to suck in your abdomen or suck in your pelvic floor, then the content sucks. (I hope all of these well-placed puns are landing.)

I don't care if they talk about "breathing correctly" or "neutral posture" or "diaphragm and pelvic floor working together." Sure, they're talking a good game. But if they're telling you to pull in your pelvic floor when you exhale and then telling you that that's the time when you ought to do the hardest part of your workout, then they're missing the boat. I almost omitted this chapter because it seems redundant after having already addressed the not-sucking-in thing, but after explaining all the breathing, posture, and core activation things to patients, they still ask about *when* to breathe and when to move. I guess we need some more repetitions here.

The reason why people say to do this (in addition to the discussion of the last chapter) is because we still have this mentality that concentric contraction (shortening) of a muscle is the only way to stabilize.

Let's pretend that you need to move a couch. This would require your pelvic floor to have an increase in load because you are taking weight onto your body. It's not just picking up the couch and therefore adding load onto your body (including your pelvic floor). You also need to move the couch. This requires unilateral (one-sided) movement with a bilateral (both-sided) load. The muscles in your arms, legs, core, and pelvic floor will do different things depending on which leg is standing and which leg is shuffle-stepping as you maneuver the couch to whatever space it needs to go (hopefully not up or down a set of stairs because that's just brutal).

If you took the training methodology of doing the hardest part of your activity while you were exhaling, you would either never move the couch or pass out while doing so. There's not really an option to do something as dynamic as moving an odd object while only exhaling. And when I put it that way, it actually sounds kind of ridiculous. But plenty of people will take that idea into a treatment room or even into a lifting session and perform the hardest part of their workout while exhaling.

Since it's not translatable to everyday life, it seems unnecessary to incorporate it into training.

One of my favorite researchers to contribute to the world of prenatal exercise is James Clapp III. In his book *Exercising Through Your Pregnancy*, he specifically mentions using your breathing to assist with weightlifting during pregnancy. He says to exhale as you lift and inhale as you return to the start position.[1] I love Dr. Clapp's work, and I recommend all providers and coaches who work with pregnant women read his book. At the same time, I cannot get behind this recommendation, and it's something that's in his book that's not specifically cited. It's just stated. (As an evidence-informed provider, I don't mind this, I'm just pointing out that it's not something that's well-researched anyway.)

This is likely because the idea comes from the idea of *tightening* the core for stability, which is the exact opposite of what the DNS model teaches. I prefer the DNS model for reasons I've already stated, but the basis of it is one of how humans are supposed to move. The other version - the tightening of the abdomen, sucking in the pelvic floor, and concentric contraction focused model - requires us to learn new ways of moving that aren't already part of our built-in human program.

By built-in human program, I mean, for example, that babies aren't taught how to roll over: they do this as part of their normal development. The same is true for crawling, sitting, and walking (please do not "sit" your babies before they can sit or "walk" your babies before they can walk).[2] Babies don't suck in their bellies to crawl. They learn to stabilize through curiosity of achieving new movements and demonstrate doing so with an expansive stabilization strategy. This is an example of why I utilize the DNS model for teaching movement and rehabilitating patients.

Maybe you'll argue that a baby's proportions are different from an adult's. (I've yet to meet anyone who argues this, but it's what I'd argue if I was arguing against this approach; I like to know the ins and outs of my stances and where they fall short.) A baby's head is about a quarter of the height of their whole body. You would look super weird if your head was still proportionally that large. To lug around that big noggin, you'd have to move differently in order to prevent yourself from falling over. But I would argue that as your body proportionally catches up to your head's size, your stabilization improves because your movements have influenced how you stabilize and vice versa.

One argument I actually have heard was in a fairly popular "core restoration" class that I took to get an idea of what that method was about. I'd heard good things about it, so I was interested. I'm paraphrasing off memory from several years ago, but the instructor said that lots of people belly breathe (as in Buddha belly) because they've been told to breathe like a baby, and that breathing like a baby is wrong. She said babies aren't good breathers and their posture isn't one we should emulate because they have their backs arched and bellies sticking out. (The instructor went on to teach some amount of resisting outward expansion of the abdomen and contracting on exhale.)

It seems to me that she threw the baby out with the bathwater on this one. I don't tell people to breathe or stand like toddlers, but I do frequently encourage them to revisit their innate movement patterns: lie on their back and lift their legs into the air, roll over while keeping their diaphragm parallel with their pelvic floor, lie on their belly and lift their head as they did in tummy time, crawl, bear crawl, and squat. These are all movements that babies do in their first year+ of life that help them establish an upright posture and help them fully develop the postural functions of their diaphragm and their core.

Most faulty breathing patterns happen into the chest, not the abdomen, although people will often overcorrect by bringing their breath forward into their abdomen when cued to stop breathing into their shoulders. My point is that I think the instructor was seeing the fault of improper compensation: when people found out that they weren't supposed to breathe into their chest, they started breathing into the front of their belly. Neither is correct, and I agree with her that I don't want people to breathe in either of those patterns.

I actually used to say "belly breathing" simply to draw awareness to expanding the abdomen, but the result was that these patients would breathe - you guessed it - into the front of their belly. Then I started to say "diaphragmatic breathing" to emphasize the primary breathing muscle and encourage breath into the back as well. I will usually use that or the terminology of a "full core breath" that I heard my co-instructor Dr. Erica Boland use.

But maybe I'm wrong. (Per my disclaimer at the beginning of the book, I reserve the right to change my mind.) Maybe this isn't the best method for rehabilitating a pelvic floor (or anything else for that matter). I have a very large bias because I've been practicing this way for over a decade and have incredible mentors who have been practicing way longer. We see really great results. But one thing that causes bias among healthcare providers is that we don't usually see our failures.

If a patient stops coming to see me unexpectedly (they have an appointment, cancel it, and never reschedule it), I typically reach out to them. But if they don't respond, I have no way of knowing if they feel great, crappy, or are just so busy living their life that going to the chiropractor hasn't made it onto their schedule. I used to take this personally and assume they obviously hated me or I'd done something horribly wrong in their care. But after being in practice for a few years, people would come back in after being MIA for a while and be so delighted to be under care again that I stopped feeling like every patient who left my office was a failure on my part.

Some of them probably were. Some of those patients who stopped coming in probably didn't get better under my care. They probably didn't see the results they were looking for. Maybe that's because they didn't do their exercises, or I didn't offer the right treatment at the right time or we just weren't the right fit for each other. But that means that they probably went to another provider of some sort. *That* provider will see my failure, not me.

I see other provider's failures. I see the ones who left the care of a PT who had them doing kegels and butterfly stretches and (not surprisingly) they still leak urine when they sneeze. I see the ones who have been doing kegels for 20+ years and are content with their dark colored leggings and frequent trips to the bathroom during workouts because their coach says that they should squeeze everything on their exhales to help prevent leakage. These patients improve under the DNS model of care.

Let me be clear that I do not represent the entire DNS model of care. I am not an instructor for them; I am a student of their methods and honestly more of a fangirl than a spokesperson. There are lots of DNS practitioners who will approach patient care differently than me because we all have differences in our execution of these methods.

In my office, we focus on creating stability between the diaphragm and pelvic floor by utilizing a patient's own intra-abdominal pressure and bracing techniques that are based more on eccentric (lengthening) activity of the abdominal wall and torso rather than concentric. Pressurization of the core canister means that there will be less muscular activity because the internal pressure is creating stability rather than the external muscles.

I tell my patients to visualize the pressure within a can of sparkling water (because I don't want them thinking about soda), and how the pressure within the can keeps it stable. If you dent the can, it's less stable than if the whole can is pressurized and closed. This pressurized canister is what your diaphragm, pelvic floor, and entire abdominal wall create together. There is some amount of concentric activity that synchronously occurs with eccentric activity, **but our focus is on meeting the resistance of expansion rather than creating the environment of contraction.**

I want to expand on that (get it? I'm talking about expansion - so punny). For some patients who have a severe diastasis (separation of their rectus abdominis muscles), when they expand their abdomen, there's not much resistance because the linea alba and abdominal tissues have been damaged by overstretching. This lack of resistance is a problem because the response of the abdominal wall to the increase in intra-abdominal pressure (IAP) is necessary for stability. If there's nothing for the IAP (which, remember, increases with each breath) to press up against, then the pressure is dispersed and loses its effectiveness.

The same thing happens if the pelvic floor is incredibly weak or overstretched (keep in mind that tight pelvic floors are a problem as well as weak ones). There needs to be resistance to the increase in pressure. That's what the Boat Theory addresses.

That doesn't mean we abandon the increase in pressure. We can't: IAP increases with each breath. Some practitioners or coaches will caution against increasing this IAP in an effort to prevent you from "damaging your pelvic floor," but I hope you can see how silly of a recommendation that is given that the method for accomplishing this would be asphyxiation. I am therefore not advocating for you to stop increasing IAP.

I think these providers might worry that when people attempt to create stabilization using IAP, they will bear down as if straining for a bowel movement rather than brace (this is known as a Valsalva maneuver and is not the same as pressurizing with IAP). We have seen that women with incontinence have altered function of the pelvic floor whether they're trying to contract their pelvic floor or bear down.[3] Translation: they're using their pelvic floor incorrectly, so - surprise! - they use their pelvic floor incorrectly. That doesn't mean we should stop them from doing anything or oversimplify the dysfunction to one muscle group; it means we need to improve their system. These providers are well-intended, but dispersing IAP inappropriately won't injure you, per se, it will simply make it harder to stabilize appropriately and won't help you heal a diastasis or pelvic floor dysfunction.

I've written about diastasis before in my first book and on my practice blog, so I won't spend too much time here, but because the two conditions - persistent/severe diastasis and PFD - can happen concurrently, I do want to touch on diastasis.[4,5]

Diastasis rectus abdominis (DRA or simply diastasis (though diastasis means "separation" and a separation could occur elsewhere in the body; when people colloquially speak about a diastasis, it's usually this one)) is a separation between the two bellies of the rectus abdominis muscles, in the connective tissue called the linea alba. The "belly" of a muscle just refers to the biggest, meatiest part of the muscle. The rectus abdominis muscles run down the middle of the front of your abdomen: these make your six-pack muscles, regardless of whether or not you can see them. A separation between these muscles happens during pregnancy as an adaptation that is perfectly normal and can close on its own (though studies vary on when exactly that can happen - some studies say up to a year).[6] It is also present at birth for most children, and closes (meaning that the two rectus muscles come to within one finger-width apart) within the first year of life. These two situations are normal.

When a diastasis is present outside of those two normal situations, it requires retraining. Keep in mind the Mota et al. study that I shared in the last chapter because it demonstrated that diastasis worsened when participants were cued to suck in.[7] Now, before I'm accused of cherry-picking research, that study actually showed that the preferable alternative to sucking in would be to do a mini-crunch. This makes my poor chiropractor heart so sad. (A mini crunch places about 2000 Newtons of compression on the lumbar spine.)[8]

Additionally, a study by Diane Lee and Paul Hodges (I told you he did a lot of research) in 2016 showed that the narrowing of the inter-rectus distance (IRD) during a crunch was due to distortion of the linea alba, meaning that the connective tissue between the muscles got kind of sloppy during a crunch.[9] They showed that pre-activation of TrA (sucking in) stopped the IRD from decreasing (meaning the diastasis didn't get smaller), and hypothesized that it improved the mechanics of the abdomen because it maintained tension within the linea alba.

You *do* need tension within your connective tissue to be able to transfer forces between different areas of your body. A 2018 review from Polish Gynecological suggested that, while it still needs to be confirmed, an optimal strategy would be to combine the activities of the different abdominal muscles.[10] I couldn't agree more.

If you're still confused and zoned out reading this because it doesn't make sense to you, start paying attention again. The combination of these last few studies that I've shown you regarding diastasis has amounted to this: crunches (which are terrible for your spine) make the distance between your six-pack muscles get smaller but do so only because the connective tissues are essentially sort of sloppy during a crunch. Translation: don't do crunches. Sucking in doesn't allow the space between your six-pack muscles to get smaller, though researchers hypothesize that it's because tensing the TrA creates more tension across the abdomen. Translation: well, it's up to you, but if you're trying to make a diastasis smaller, I recommend avoiding something that *doesn't make a diastasis smaller*. Ipso facto, stop sucking in.

So we know that sucking in won't heal a diastasis, crunches won't heal a diastasis, and avoiding IAP is impossible to do and therefore can't help heal a diastasis. Instead, we need appropriate pressure management within the abdominal and pelvic cavity (that's just the space within the belly and pelvis, respectively). Because most people are inappropriately managing IAP, I can't give you a sure-fire example of how to feel a responsive activity of your abdominal wall when you increase IAP. My best bet is to have you feel the difference between what stabilizing your body in a responsive way feels like compared to when sucking in, so the exercise at the end of this chapter will attempt to do so.

After you have felt this activity within your body, your brain has better proprioceptive and kinesthetic awareness of how to recreate it, but your chances of success will increase if you allow yourself some intentional interoception (perception of your internal state).

Exercise - Partner Shove

This exercise requires a partner. It is an informative exercise for you that helps to explain why I don't rely on sucking in for core stabilization. It is also not at all appropriate to perform if you are less than two months postpartum or post-abdominal surgery. It's a playful exercise, but paying very close attention can make this a powerfully informative exercise as well.

Stand next to your partner with your feet hip or shoulder width apart (whichever feels more comfortable) and weight evenly distributed on both feet. Now the fun begins because I want your partner to try to push you over. Set some ground rules that there is to be no violent shoving nor any dirty tricks here, but simply have your partner lean their body into yours, primarily using the outside of their arm or shoulder to try to nudge you over. Don't block them with your hands. As you try to prevent them from knocking you off balance, use one of your hands to palpate (remember, that just means feel) your abdomen. What's it doing?

The natural response to maintaining stability is for your abdomen to expand into your hand.

Now suck in and repeat the exercise. Since we're assuming you had terrible stabilizing strategies, this will most likely be how you were typically attempting to brace yourself for a challenging lift or activity. Ask your partner to use the same amount of effort to shove you over. I don't know your partner, so I can't specifically vouch for their integrity and whether or not they're shoving you harder, but I can tell you that every single time I've done this exercise, people become increasingly easy to push over as soon as they suck in.

Now we're actually going to play around with task-specific IAP and help your brain to feel what this feels like via interoception and proprioception.

Start with a scale. Let's call your partner's effort in the last attempt 100%: they were attempting to make you lose your footing but not actually trying to take you down like a playground bully. Have them start at 100% so that you can get the feedback, and then ask them to temper their effort while you notice intentionally what changes occur in your body. This will give you an example of task-specific intra-abdominal pressure. Your IAP will change in response to your partner's efforts. How does your abdomen feel when they are offering you a 50% effort? Or 70%? Or only 20%?

Close your eyes so that you limit the external input you're getting and can focus better internally. Place your hands on your abdomen - including your sides and back - to feel the responsive activity in your abdomen and note how this feels notably different than when you are pulling in your stomach or tightening your muscles.

If you have a willing partner who wants to help you rehabilitate your pelvic floor and garner improved awareness of your internal stabilization system, feel free to let them nudge you a bit a few times a week and pay attention to your internal sensation of your natural tendency to create stability.

CHAPTER 12

SURGERY

I wish I knew who said this to me regarding surgery:

"You can't un-ring that bell."

As a chiropractor, I am focused on conservative care. This means I am as minimally invasive and am attempting to conserve things as they are - while still improving them - rather than changing how things are. The alternative would be approaching care from a more invasive standpoint: doing the most to change the current situation in order to hopefully improve it. This also means that I am far from an expert in pelvic surgery, but wish to address it since it is an option for PFD. According to a 2017 study, the lifetime risk of surgery for women with incontinence or pelvic organ prolapse is 20.5%.[1]

A wonderful pelvic health physical therapist that I work with, Dr. Kelly Raney, told me about a patient of hers who had undergone general orthopedic physical therapy for coccydynia (tailbone pain) before coming to see her. When the patient hadn't improved, a surgeon she'd been referred to recommended a coccygectomy. If you're not brushed up on your

Latin, that translates to removing the coccyx. Remember that the coccyx is the back of the pelvic floor and therefore an attachment for most of the muscles of the pelvic floor. The woman hadn't wanted to opt for surgery and found Dr. Raney, and within a few visits had no tailbone pain to speak of.

My point in relaying this story is that the surgeon likely was thinking that the patient already exhausted her conservative care options and therefore was automatically a surgical candidate. She'd tried *some* conservative options and they hadn't worked for her, which *could* mean that she ought to progress to the next level of intervention. But for this patient, surgery was far from the only option moving forward. The patient had done orthopedic PT, but not pelvic PT.

The type of tools that your doctor has available will greatly impact the type of recommendations that you get. I tell patients all the time about a prospective study of workers with low back pain. If they saw a surgeon first, 43% of those workers had surgery. If they saw a chiropractor first, 1.5% of those workers had surgery.[2] I don't opt for surgery because it's not in my wheelhouse. If I was a surgeon, I would probably lean on that tool more. I have had patients whom I've referred for surgery, but even in most surgical cases, we're able to do a trial of conservative care first.

The conservative approach is to apply care while keeping all pieces of the body intact, and not invade the body with anything foreign. If we follow the conservative care model, we will only progress a patient toward further intervention if we tried the lowest level of intervention(s) first. We would start with the most conservative option and then only progress to more invasive means of treatment when and if necessary. What follows is my model of most conservative to least conservative methods of care for musculoskeletal complaints with some basic examples; it's not than an agreed-upon definition within healthcare professions. Translation: this is an example of how I opt to approach most care. Another practitioner may have a different approach. You can identify how conservative a treatment is based on how much it changes the body.

While not technically a mode of treatment, there is one commonly overlooked option for care and that is the choice to do nothing. Inaction has risks, benefits, and side effects, but it obviously doesn't change the body, so it technically would be the most conservative option, though it's not really care.

For any musculoskeletal complaint, the most conservative care options would be things like chiropractic care, physical therapy, exercise alone, a nutrition program, or smoking cessation if that applies. These are all treatments that can be done to a body and are *done* making changes within the body after the treatment is through (though effects can last longer).

The next level of intervention would be putting something into the body that is foreign. This could be needles for acupuncture or dry needling. (Some practitioners argue that this is a purely conservative approach because the needles are a tool; I see them as invading the body, and therefore are more invasive than treatments that remain outside the body, and I therefore usually incorporate dry needling after I've already utilized other less invasive tools.) This could also be physical therapy that enters a body's orifice (such as a gloved hand to perform pelvic trigger point release or inserting a biofeedback sensor; again, many would argue that these are extremely conservative measures, but they both include a foreign object entering the body, so are technically more invasive).

Another option under this mostly conservative heading would be a nutraceutical or pharmaceutical prescription: supplements specifically targeted toward changing physiology to address a symptom (as opposed to supplements that generally support the body broadly), or a drug (over the counter or prescription) that would change the body's chemistry to address a symptom. There are varying degrees of drugs: some are stronger than others and have greater effects. Like in the most conservative option, these interventions are *done* when the treatment is done; in the case of drugs or supplements, the treatment would be completely over after it has worked through the body's detoxification systems.

The next level of non-surgical intervention would be akin to an injection of physiological agents (such as PRP) or drugs into the area of concern. PRP (platelet-rich plasma) injections take the body's own blood (after it is withdrawn and centrifuged) and inject it into the area of injury to stimulate healing. Though limited research exists, it has been shown to be promising for PFD.[3,4] Drug injections could be something like a corticosteroid injection (anti-inflammatory drug); or a procedure such as a nerve block. These treatments are *done* after the injection wears off. In the case of PRP, it's simply the body's blood, so it integrates fairly seamlessly. In a nerve block or drug injection, the drug wears off and runs through the body's detoxification systems in a similar way to oral medications.

The final option is surgery. There are levels of invasiveness: some surgeries are more invasive than others (don't forget that laparoscopic doesn't mean less invasive to the body, it just has less scar tissue that's visible). Once you do surgery, there is no going back to not having done surgery, and even though the operation is *over*, the surgery isn't *done*. You changed parts of the body surgically. If you remove parts, they don't grow back the same. If you add hardware, they're there forever. The scars are now a new addition as well. This isn't to say that's a bad thing: sometimes surgery is absolutely necessary. Regardless, you can't un-ring that bell.

All our choices have consequences. In healthcare, we typically call these side effects. When I start to think of them as consequences, that seems to make them more real. The laundry list of side effects people hear after a pharmaceutical commercial make them think that side effects are rare or unlikely, but there are always consequences to what we choose to do. This is another good reminder that awareness brings choice. Choice is better than no choice.

Some practitioners are more invasive than others. They'll opt for surgery way faster than others. Most practitioners recognize the benefit of conservative care for the same reason that if you can use a hammer to get a job done, you wouldn't use a crane.

An easy way to demonstrate this is with treatment for back pain, since lots of people have low back pain and seek lots of different treatments for it. In one prospective randomized clinical study, 60% of patients with sciatica from a lumbar disc herniation who failed other medical management (including drugs, physiotherapy, lifestyle modification, massage, and acupuncture - all of which are variations of conservative care) benefited from spinal manipulation to the same degree as if they underwent surgical intervention. That study stated in its conclusion that these patients should consider spinal manipulation and can go on to surgery if necessary.[5] We can always go on to more invasive types of intervention, but the reverse is not always true.

Within the pelvic floor, there are various surgeries that can be performed. Some have the intention of reconstructing the pelvic floor organs, muscles, and ligaments as in the case of pelvic organ prolapse. Others have the intention of supporting the urethra to reduce incontinence. Hysterectomy and prostatectomy would also fall under pelvic surgeries.

Regarding prostatectomy, since I'm not sexist and there are men reading this book: as of a 2015 prospective, controlled, nonrandomized trial, greater than 20% of prostatectomy patients reported incontinence one year after surgery, regardless of surgery type. In the same study, greater than 70% of men reported erectile dysfunction at one year post-op.[6]

The most common pelvic surgeries for pelvic organ prolapse and other non-malignant pelvic disorders involve mesh reconstruction of some sort. A common intervention for stress urinary incontinence is a mid-urethral sling of mesh.

A 2016 Cochrane Review of RCTs comparing outcomes of permanent mesh, absorbable mesh, and native tissue repair for vaginal prolapse showed that transvaginal mesh had limited utility because of its risk-benefit profile and absorbable mesh could reduce recurrent prolapse (but limited evidence existed for this). The review also noted the voluntary recall in 2011 of many transvaginal permanent meshes.[7]

In more recent years, the FDA issued a recall of all surgical mesh in 2019 that was intended for transvaginal repair of POP due to safety concerns.[8] Not all mesh was problematic, and doctors continue to use mesh for mid-urethral slings.

A Danish national database study of 1657 women who underwent pelvic organ prolapse surgery showed that over 70% of women reported full continence or improvements in continence.[9] A Finnish prospective nationwide study out of 2351 participants showed health-related quality of life was improved two years post-surgery in seven out of ten women.[10] It's worth noting that this study specifically mentioned that smoking cessation was necessary to avoid an unfavorable outcome. This further emphasizes my point that a lot of factors play into pelvic floor health: smoking doesn't directly cause

PFD, but if you're a smoker and have PFD, reparative surgery goes better if you quit.

A Cochrane Review shows that there's little evidence to support pre-operative treatment of the pelvic floor muscles via therapy, but the evidence wasn't strong and was only based on two small studies.[11] Despite this, many providers prefer to have patients undergo pre-operative care to some extent to help prepare the patient's body for surgery, or in some instances, avoid surgery altogether.

There is one surgery that's not specifically done to the pelvic floor but has shown benefit for PFD: bariatric surgery in obese adults. A 2017 meta-analysis showed significant improvements of PFD in obese women who underwent bariatric surgery, though no statistically significant improvements in fecal incontinence or sexual function were found.[12]

Some patients have been told that they are surgical candidates, but don't want to undergo the risks of surgery and therefore opt for a lower quality of life. There are a variety of less invasive options to consider other than surgery when it comes to caring for the pelvic floor, and a little creativity along the path might actually divert a patient from surgery. If it doesn't, then perhaps surgery will be wildly successful. If it's not, then post-surgical rehabilitation can yield further improvements. In one RCT, there was a small statistically significant improvement in patients who had one preoperative and five postoperative sessions of pelvic floor exercise and behavioral therapy for a mid-urethral sling procedure.[13]

There are plenty of options and most patients can expect to see improvements with some form of therapy. Your pelvic floor doesn't have to suck forever. If surgery is necessary, I encourage you to exhaust all options before making that determination and ensure that your recovery includes everything we're covering in this book.

Happy **Unexpected** Results

Testimonial

I went to see Dr Mumma as a new patient because of chronic lower back and intermittent neck pain. I have suffered for at least 10 years - never debilitating… but close. My husband was seeing her as a patient with positive results, so I decided to take a chance.

During the first visit she asked a lot of questions and examined me more thoroughly than my regular doctor. We broached the topic of pelvic floor issues. I complained that I also have these issues (leaking when running or sneezing). She explained it isn't something I had to live with. She not only helped me with my back issues but also (surprisingly) with my leaking. I am a mom who last gave birth 20 years ago… so old moms can get help too! I went to see Mumma (as I call her) to help with my back pain and I came out receiving a lot more than I expected. She's amazing!

*- **Michele S.***

Exercise - Make an Appointment

Go see a chiropractor. If you don't have one, visit MotionPalpation.org and check their referral list. Or just ask your friends. People generally love their chiropractors and are thrilled that you're just as weird as them and want to see a chiropractor, too.

If your chiropractor doesn't have a specialty in treatment of pelvic floor disorders, they can still help you simply because they can improve your biomechanics, which - as we've addressed at length - has impacts on your pelvic floor in very specific ways. (And here's another shameless plug to gift them a copy of this book.) Chiropractic care is one form of conservative care that is simply worth trying. I'm incredibly biased in this recommendation. If you're already seeing a chiropractor (yay!), then you don't get off easy on this chapter. Your exercise is to go see a pelvic PT or an acupuncturist. If you see all of them, then go meet with a shaman.

PART 4

A WHOLE LIFE APPROACH TO PELVIC FLOOR HEALTH

CHAPTER 13

NUTRITION FOR YOUR PELVIC FLOOR

A lot of people cringe when they hear the word "nutrition," but before you get all cringey, let's define it. My friend Mel Hemphill (who is currently in school to become a pelvic PT and might already be practicing when you are reading this book, so you should look her up) helped expand my definition several years ago when she exposed me to Eating Psychology and the work of Marc David. Since then, I've considered how what we surround ourselves with and take in or absorb can be sources of "nutrition." This can include food, beverages, people, pollutants, toxins, media, fabrics, personal care products, rest, and even thoughts. With that broad definition, let's explore how nutrition can impact your pelvic floor health.

But before we do, I'm going to start with one of the most random-seeming nutrition recommendations I give to women to help support their pelvic floor: spraying a soil derivative on it.

One way that I've found to help bring balance to the vaginal flora (the beneficial bacteria that live in the vagina) and speed healing in the postpartum time period is by using ION* Skin Support. Let me be very clear that this is completely off-label use of this supplemental skin spray and has not been approved by the company. But it's been so helpful for myself and lots of patients that I feel compelled to share it with you. ION stands for Intelligence of Nature and it's a liquid gut support supplement created by Dr. Zach Bush that I recommend for lots of my patients because of its ability to help restore balance within the gut by sealing cells within the gut lining. When they came out with their skin spray that was intended to help support the skin's functions, I started using it right away on my face and body. (I'm generally interested in n=1 experiments, meaning that there's one subject in this particular scientific study, and that subject is me.)

After I personally had pelvic floor PRP injections (because n=1), I used the ION* Skin Support on my own perineum to calm down the post-injection inflammation and help my tissues heal. It worked really well, so I started recommending it to my postpartum patients. (Spraying the perineum with cooling herbal mists is a common practice for postpartum women (ingredients like witch hazel, lavender, aloe, and calendula are frequently used in sprays or made into "padsicles," which are frozen sanitary pads with those ingredients poured onto them - these can also be helpful for a sore scrotum after a vasectomy), so this isn't as weird sounding as you might think.) I tell women to spritz their nether regions with ION* Skin Support after they get out of the shower.

Is spraying a soil-derived skin support product on your perineum going to solve your PFD? Likely no. But is it going to contribute to an overall improved microbiome, which will contribute to an overall healthy you, which will contribute to the ability for your pelvic floor to function optimally? Likely yes.

Health of the pelvic floor is obviously going to be dependent upon the health of the tissues themselves, which includes their blood flow, lymphatic flow, tissue pliability, cellular turnover, lubrication, and balance of bacteria. All these functions are impacted by (the broad definition of) nutrition.

Dietary Intake

Let's shift focus to where most people begin in terms of nutrition: dietary intake. I've briefly mentioned the importance of an anti-inflammatory diet, and I want to expand upon it further. An anti-inflammatory diet is one that actively decreases inflammation and concurrently doesn't promote it. I tell my patients that an anti-inflammatory diet, according to the work of Dr. David Seaman, comprises five categories: fruits, vegetables, meats, nuts, and fish.[1] Conveniently, there are five categories and I have five fingers, so I count them out on each finger.

I tell patients that if the food they are eating is categorized as one of the aforementioned, eat whatever they'd like. If the food they're eating isn't in one of those categories, then eat only condiment-sized portions of that food. I'm not talking about the amount of ketchup that my sons use because that is astronomical, but a normal condiment-sized portion for an adult with no specific affinity for condiments. You may notice that the foods not listed would include grains, dairy, and sugars.

Some people tolerate dairy better than others, and full fat dairy with no added sugar has great benefits. But unpasteurized, non-homogenized A2 dairy is hard to find and, in many states, illegal for humans to consume. (I'm not a fan of the government telling you what you can and cannot consume, for the record.) Fermented dairy like kefir, cottage cheese, and yogurt can all be beneficial for gut flora if you can tolerate dairy products and have an intact gut lining.

In the same way, some people tolerate the consumption of grains better than others, but minimizing processed grains isn't going to hurt anyone because the minimal nutrients available from grains can be easily gathered from other sources of plants and animals.

Other influential voices in my nutrition recommendation wheelhouse include Dr. Mark Hyman; Mark Sisson; Max Lugavere; Dr. James Chestnut; Lily Nichols, RDN; and Dr. Weston A. Price. All of them have published various books, articles, blogs, and podcasts that are worth investigating if you wish to learn more about nutrition.

If most of the time your diet is anti-inflammatory, your overall health can improve. I'm trying to help you get the building blocks in order so that your pelvic floor can do what it's supposed to do. Part of that is relying on your food to fuel you rather than hinder your progress. Perhaps it is helpful for you to think of food as information: telling your body what to do. Even thinking of food as medicine can be helpful. Dr. Hyman published a two-part article entitled *Food, Medicine, and Function: Food is Medicine.*[2] It is a great resource to dive further into the topic. In so many words, food can either create the internal environment for health, or it can create an environment for disease. Additionally, the foods that you eat give you fuel and energy you need to be able to accomplish tasks efficiently. This includes tissue repair, building strength, and improving health.

Not specific to the pelvic floor, but a 2022 study showed that taking collagen peptides when paired with resistance training showed improved recovery, decreased pain, and improved strength and body composition.[3] All of the above would contribute to healing of pelvic floor tissues (including the resistance training). This brings up a really important point for you if you're a vegetarian or Vegan.

Supplementation

Collagen is abundant in animal sources, but not so in plant sources. Vitamin B12 is similar. Vegans are more likely to have decreased levels of B12, which increases the risk of bone fracture.[4] Low B12 levels have also been linked with depression, specifically during pregnancy.[5] Your neuromusculoskeletal system requires adequate collagen and B12 to function fully. If you're not eating animal sources of nutrition, then frequent lab tests to determine your exact supplemental needs is a wise choice.

Supplements can be very beneficial to your overall health but shouldn't replace your dietary intake of nutrients. Let's discuss a few supplemental additions to your diet that may be beneficial for your pelvic floor. (I have links to these recommendations in the Resources at the end of the book as well.) The first is ION* Biome's Gut Support, which is taken orally before meals. This is the actual on-label use recommendation of this product, though I do also obviously recommend the spray as well.

Adequate nutrients can help your body perform its functions optimally. Methylated B vitamins, omega-3s, collagen, and adaptogenic herbs are all frequent recommendations I give to patients to do just that. I generally also recommend an organ complex for patients who aren't regularly consuming offal (the internal organs of an animal when used as food), especially in the postpartum time period to help replenish lost nutrients.

I frequently recommend adding supplemental electrolytes, as this makes water more hydrating. Electrolytes are charged minerals like sodium, potassium, calcium, and magnesium that you rely on for multiple functions in your body. Many people are drinking adequate (or even too much) water without replenishing the electrolytes that they lose through their sweat, urine, or bowel movements. I personally enjoy LMNT every day, which tastes like salty Gatorade.

Another form of hydration that accomplishes a similar objective is to make herbal infusions. Susun Weed is an herbalist who showcased the idea of making incredibly strong herbal tea (stinging nettles is one of my favorites) using one ounce of herbs in a quart of hot water and leaving them to steep for at least four hours before cooling and consuming. I drink herbal infusions daily and have a video tutorial from Susun Weed in your Resources if you'd like to try them yourself.

Coffee is a known bladder irritant, so sometimes eliminating or limiting it can be helpful for calming down PFD symptoms. There are many coffee alternatives, but I encourage patients who are forgoing their morning cup of Joe to swap it for a cup of bone broth so they have a hot beverage with lots of nutrients to start their day.

One final note on hydration would be to investigate the water you're drinking. Tap water is full of a litany of chemicals that add up over time as you consume them. Filtering your water can go a long way toward supporting better health. I also choose structured water (water that is the same structure as that found in springs and other natural sources before it's taken through chemical filtering). We have an incredible water station at my practice that structures the water after filtering, but you can do this by simply stirring it. Consuming structured water has been shown in animal studies to improve overall markers of health.[6] Animal studies aren't the same as human studies, but in another n=1 experiment, I feel much better drinking filtered, structured water, and it just tastes better anyway.

Gut Function and Key Factors

What you do, how you eat, what you drink, and how you behave greatly impact your overall health and the health of your tissues. Supporting your gut function can help you better digest and utilize the nutrients you're taking in. (This is why I love ION*.) The ability to improve digestion in any capacity has impacts on the ability of the pelvic floor to do one of its main functions of excreting waste. As your gut health improves, your ability to eliminate waste can become easier. If you suffer from constipation, IBS, diarrhea, or straining for bowel movements, your pelvic floor is likely taking a bit of a beating.

One proctologist told a patient of mine - who visited him after she started having mucous in her stools - that what she ate couldn't influence her bowel movements. I am still flabbergasted by this statement from nearly ten years ago and have high hopes that this doctor has since grown in his clinical observations and recommendations. I said a lot of dumb stuff ten years ago, too. In the simplest of terms, what goes in gets broken down and used, if possible, and the waste products are sent out the other end. What *else* could influence your bowel movements more than the food that you directly put into your gastrointestinal (GI) system?

At the completely opposite end is the start of your GI system. We've talked about jaw health, but the mouth plays another important role in pelvic floor health from the standpoint of nutrition because it's the starting point of digestion (technically your brain starts digestion, but let's not get too far into the weeds, eh?). Your saliva and the bacteria within your mouth begin to break down the food that you eat. Lots of people are swishing mouthwash to kill the bacteria that's responsible for beginning digestion, and then taking a probiotic to help restore normal gut flora (AKA gut bacteria). Wouldn't it make sense to *not* kill those bacteria to start with?

I'm not advocating that you stop brushing your teeth, but the work of Weston A. Price (a dentist who recognized that narrower faces were leading to health problems and that they were the result of poor nutrition) showed that once less nutrient-dense foods (such as sugar, flour, pasteurized milk, and preservative-filled convenience foods) were introduced to cultures, their offspring began to show tooth decay and crowding.[7] In cultures where toothbrushing wasn't present but neither were fake foods, people had beautiful, pristine smiles with plenty of space for all of their teeth - including their wisdom teeth!

I don't know many people who have their wisdom teeth, and I find it strange that it's commonplace to have too many parts in your body and need to have some of them surgically removed as you reach adulthood. My hope is that my kids (or at least their children, if they have any) can keep all of their teeth because their bone structure can support it. Just to be clear, I do brush my teeth at least twice per day. Most of the time I use a prebiotic toothpaste called Revitin that cleans my teeth but doesn't kill the beneficial bacteria in my mouth. I ditched traditional mouthwashes about a decade ago, but occasionally I'll use a neem oil-based mouth rinse or a mineral mouth rinse.

Dr. Price's work focused on prenatal nutrition and its impact on offspring, even noting the common practices of both partners preparing for birth months and years before conceiving in many traditional cultures. This not only helped form their babies appropriately, but could also contribute to better healing in the postpartum time period.[7] The book *The Postnatal Depletion Cure* by Dr. Oscar Serrallach covers the variety of ways that women can become depleted in the postpartum time period, and how failing to replenish basic nutrients can lead to increased healing times.[8] (For the record, the exercises in the book are fairly terrible - lots of sucking in - but the information is otherwise wonderful.)

A 2020 RCT comparing women who received only a prenatal vitamin for the first six weeks postpartum compared to those who received a formula of prenatal vitamin plus omega-3 fatty acids, zinc, and leucine showed improvements in pelvic floor recovery following vaginal birth in the additional nutrient group.[9] The addition of nutrients helped to maximize the body's healing capabilities.

I briefly talked about the vaginal microbiome. The bacteria living in your vagina need to be there to prevent infections like bacterial vaginosis or Group B *streptococcus* (GBS) colonization during pregnancy. The prominent beneficial bacteria found in normal healthy women in the vagina is *lactobacillus*.[10] A prospective case-control study showed that vaginal insertion of tablets of probiotic *lactobacillus rhamnosus* showed improvements all the way up to nine months post-bacterial vaginosis.[11] Taking oral probiotics containing *lactobacillus rhamnosus* and *lactobacillus reuteri* have been shown to decrease GBS colonization in pregnant women.[12]

One study showed a significant decrease in the likelihood of pelvic floor dysfunction in women with increasing vitamin D levels.[13] I typically recommend sunshine over supplementing with vitamin D, but also know that not many people are getting appropriate sun exposure to produce adequate vitamin D. Vitamin D is created in the body when we're exposed to UVB rays from the sun, which I recommend you do on a daily basis. I actually recommend you intentionally view (without sunglasses or corrective lenses) the sun's rays at sunrise, midday, and sunset to help improve your vitamin D levels and normalize your circadian rhythm (wake-sleep cycle).[14] Light exposure can also improve sexual function in men.[15] (Look, I mentioned men again.)

All these elements are important for pelvic floor health, healing, and function, but they're not the only nutritional inputs into your system. The movement of blood and lymph throughout your body is a source of nutrition: this brings oxygenated blood and removes waste products. If you're sitting all day, your circulation decreases, but interrupting sitting with light activity helps prevent those deleterious effects.[16]

A few notes regarding exposure: the fabrics of your undergarments can potentially impact vaginal flora due to the breathability of the fabric, though this isn't well-supported by research. Phthalates are endocrine disrupting compounds that are used in personal care products and as plasticizers in a variety of everyday objects, and as such, if you are exposed regularly to phthalates, this can impact your hormonal health and overall health.[17] We previously touched on tampon use and the potential exposure to chemicals in the vagina.

We've already discussed how stress impacts your pelvic floor, so I hope you can sense the importance of how the people you surround yourself with, your own thoughts, and the media you consume can all contribute to an upregulated or downregulated autonomic nervous system (ANS). These can either be nutritious sources or can lack nutritional value. Your overall nutrition impacts your overall health.

Nutrient Timing

Another tool that my friend Mel Hemphill shared with me from her work as an Eating Psychology Practitioner was to take ten deep breaths before eating. This helps downregulate the ANS, which then primes the brain and body for the task of digestion. It also gives you an extra thirty intentional breaths per day if you do it before breakfast, lunch, and dinner.

A quick note on three meals per day: intermittent fasting (IF) is lauded by some as the cure-all for all metabolic and mental health issues while being condemned by others for hormone dysregulation and disordered eating. As usual, the truth is likely to be found somewhere between these two extremes. If you're not familiar, the idea of intermittent fasting is to have periods of not eating (fasting) followed by periods of eating (hence: intermittent). In general, people will typically choose an "eating window" that is somewhere between 4-12 hours, and a fasting window that is between 20-12 hours, respectively.

There's not great data on the specifics of IF as it relates to pelvic floor function. But there is evidence that intermittent fasting can contribute to improving insulin sensitivity in women (meaning it would improve health by making the body more appropriately sensitive to insulin).[18] Conversely, women with insulin resistance (meaning your body is not appropriately sensitive to insulin) have less muscle activity in their pelvic floor.[19]

I have experimented with intermittent fasting on and off for about five years. Please remember that this is an n=1 study of one person and therefore akin to an anecdote, not an actual study. I'm just sharing my experience.

One thing IF helped me with was to break up habitual eating: eating at specific times because it was "time to eat" or simply because food was available. I started to ask myself before eating if I was actually hungry. I know, it was quite a novel idea, and one that I've kept with me even when I'm not fasting.

The first time that I intentionally did IF, I was tandem nursing my sons (meaning both of my sons were breastfeeding at the time), when I was around ten months postpartum. I was nearly constantly hungry. I did not feel like I could eat enough to satiate me, no matter what my food intake was. I was eating plenty of nutrient-dense foods, but I was still hungry most of the time. I wasn't gaining or losing any weight but maintaining my same weight. I decided that since I was already hungry, I would try to be intentionally hungry and see what happened.

Surprisingly, it helped break up my persistent sense of hunger. The first time I did IF, I ate dinner, skipped breakfast and the initial urge to eat, at which point I didn't feel hungry. I felt a change in my hunger a little after mid-day, so I ate a late lunch. For the first time since giving birth, I felt full after eating.

I don't outright recommend IF, but it can be a useful tool. I did find benefit in my ability to differentiate hunger cues from other cues I'd attached to being hungry like boredom, habit, or even loneliness. This is another instance of improving awareness that helped improve function. Remember: awareness brings choice; choice is better than no choice. This is also another one of those examples where improving one aspect of awareness or health could tangentially improve pelvic floor function.

Sleep

The final aspect of nutrition that I want to introduce is your sleep quality. Sleep can either be nutritious or not, and ideally your sleep cycles are long enough that you are able to rest and repair overnight. Your circadian rhythm determines your wake-sleep cycles and the timing of hormone release that helps your body function appropriately throughout the day as well as throughout your menstrual cycle if you have one. According to a 2020 Review, sleep deprivation is associated with depression, hypertension, glucose deregulation, cardiovascular disease, and anxiety disorders.[20]

Similarly, disrupting this cycle (largely through shift work) is related to a decreased fertility in both men and women, as well as increasing the "stress hormone," cortisol. This can decrease testosterone production in both sexes and cause excessive Hypothalamus-Pituitary Adrenal (HPA) activation, which can result in early pregnancy loss, failed embryo implantation, anovulation (lack of ovulation), and amenorrhea (missing periods). Sleep deprivation has also been shown to reduce secretion of female sex hormones in post-menopausal women.[20] In other words, sleep significantly impacts hormonal health throughout the life cycle.

Prioritizing sleep can be a challenge for many, but introducing a few habits can make a significant impact. Attempt to mimic the sun's activity because, as discussed, your exposure to sunlight will impact your circadian rhythm. I self-impose a "no-computer after 8pm" rule that I follow pretty strictly, and then I back up my own accountability by putting our Wi-Fi on a Christmas light timer. (If you don't celebrate Christmas, then it's just a timer that you plug things into, but I literally bought it in the section of the store with Christmas lights for sale.) The timer automatically shuts the Wi-Fi off at 8:30pm and then turns it back on at 5:30am. Not only am I not going to be using my tech devices after 8:30, but it also means less radiofrequency exposure in my house while my body and brain are attempting to rest and repair, which helps me sleep more soundly.

I also notice that when my nutrient intake is more robust, I sleep better. I encourage my patients who are having a hard time sleeping to add omega-3s and an organ complex supplement to improve their nutrient intake before suggesting melatonin. Melatonin is a hormone. When used in small quantities, it can be very helpful, but it can also signal to the brain that there is adequate melatonin available and therefore encourage a decreased production of this hormone. So, while many suggest it as a "natural" alternative to the hypnotic drugs like zolpidem and the litany of side effects that come along with them for the treatment of insomnia, I prefer to encourage better nutrient uptake and improved sleep hygiene.

Sleep hygiene would include low lights at night, a calming or relaxing evening routine leading up to bedtime, no or low blue light exposure after the sun sets*, and having a

---

* It is important to note that while blue light blockers have become quite popular and they are very helpful for offsetting the extreme levels of blue light we are exposed to during this technological age, it is absolutely imperative that you *are* exposed to blue light during the day. My MD (remember her? She recommends being a human *being?*) told me she had a few patients with a new onset of depression after getting blue light blocking lenses put into their prescription glasses. I have since shared her recommendation against getting blue light blocking lenses if you wear your glasses all day. Instead, get add-on blue light blocking lenses or wrap-around glasses to wear for extensive computer work that you can then remove and be able to see using your prescriptive lenses. Sure, you might not look as cool, but you could decrease your risk of developing seasonal affective disorder (SAD) or depression by exposing yourself to the full light spectrum, which is

consistent sleep schedule (going to bed and getting up around the same time every day - even on weekends).

As much as I want to encourage your completion of this book, if you're reading it after dark, it may be time to set the book down and pick it up tomorrow during the daytime. I'll still be here. (Is that creepy to say?) Either way, don't forget to do the exercise before you move on to the next chapter.

Exercise - Finger Suck

I thought about making your exercise for this chapter to be consuming an anti-inflammatory diet, but that's more of a life goal than a chapter goal. I legitimately want you to eat foods that nourish your body and improve your health, which will improve your pelvic floor function. I also want you to have lots of exercises in your wheelhouse that you can tap into, and the book is only so long.

So instead, you're going to suck on your finger. That's probably not even the strangest thing I've said so far in this book. This is another exercise that I learned from Martina Ježková at a DNS Women's Health course. We'll do this both in lying and seated, but let's start with lying down. Oh, and wash your hands.

Begin on your back with your knees bent and feet flat on the floor like we've done before. Relax your body as much as possible and pay very close attention to your pelvic floor. This is a really subtle exercise, so you need to tune in as much

necessary for your overall health. Alternatively, programs like f.lux can be downloaded to your computer to apply a blue light filter to your screen.

as possible. Place either the very tip of your thumb or the back of the middle knuckle on your first finger* into your mouth, just past your teeth (but not like a typical image of someone sucking on their thumb).

Seal your lips gently around your finger/thumb tip and gently suck. You don't need to go to town, just create gentle suction and *notice* your pelvic floor. There is an ever-so-subtle lift of the pelvic floor that occurs when you create a closed suction within your abdominal cavity. This is not an active contraction, just a response to the suction you've created.

You may not be able to feel a thing when you do this. If you can't, that's okay. It might actually be easier to try this seated. Come to a seated position in an upright neutral posture with your ischial tuberosities underneath you (your "butt bones," not your tailbone). Recreate the sealed suction and pay attention to your pelvic floor. If you can't notice anything, then now is a good time to revisit the exercise of sitting on your fingertips to get some more proprioceptive input of what your pelvic floor is doing.

Revisit this exercise once per week to create awareness and to experience a functional lifting of the pelvic floor that isn't a kegel.

---

* Health would be so much less mystifying if we conversed about things in a language that everyone could understand. If you happen to be familiar with anatomical terms, the dorsal DIP joint on your second phalanx works well for this exercise.

CHAPTER 14

AVOIDING INFODEMENTIA

Thus far, we've covered the basics of anatomy and the importance of your breath and posture - head to toe. We talked about how most people don't even recognize symptoms of PFD, and what problems can arise with it. We've talked about contributing, concurrent, and confounding factors to PFD such as pain, prolapse, scar tissue, and lack of proprioception. And we've exhausted the list of things that don't work that well or maybe sometimes sort of work.

My hope is that this information hasn't overwhelmed you, but has prepared you for applying what we've covered so far in a way that will allow you to actually succeed in improving your pelvic floor function. The alternative would be that you've now just gotten a lot of information and have no idea what to do with it. This is called infodementia.

Infodementia isn't a real thing, per se, but it's an important made-up term. Sometimes you have so much information that you can't fully grasp anything in particular that's useful. My late kundalini yoga (we'll talk about that in a second) teacher, Guru Jagat, talked about this and specifically used this term. And Dr. Winchester is quoted as saying that students (referring to chiropractic students) are "drowning in information but are starving for application."

We've already implemented exercises that intentionally set the stage so that by the time you got to this point, you'd be ready to undertake the next ones. That means if you've been reading the book and not performing the exercises, then, in my best Gandalf impression: *you shall not pass*.

I obviously have no control over your actions, nor do I want it because freedom is a value of mine and I therefore value yours. I do want you to benefit from reading this book (so that you can then write a five-star review about how great your experience was, of course) rather than just hypothetically considering the activities. I haven't published research yet because it's not been a priority for me to do so. I just have experience personally and have witnessed the experiences of hundreds of others who have taken the steps in this book to improve their pelvic floor function. I want you to be one of those success stories (and not just selfishly for the book reviews, I promise).

I put a pin in the term "kundalini yoga" for this purpose. Lots of exercises in kundalini yoga consist of pulling a root lock, which means to draw the pelvic floor up and in, along with the lower abdomen. I began doing kundalini yoga when I was around two months postpartum at the recommendation of my Naturopathic Doctor. She wanted me to use it as a stress-relieving practice at the very beginning of my journey toward being diagnosed with (and subsequently healing) two autoimmune conditions. I loved it and have practiced fairly regularly since the end of 2016.

I was dealing with pelvic floor dysfunction, though it wasn't stress incontinence like most women experience in the postpartum time period. Regardless, I still didn't want to challenge my pelvic floor with repetitive squeezing and lifting in the early postpartum months the way that the practice of kundalini yoga recommended. I didn't start doing this type of concentric contraction of my pelvic floor and lower abdomen until around ten months postpartum, at which point it felt good to have the full energetic practice of moving energy in my body from root to crown chakra, but didn't cause any undue stress on my healing tissues in the postpartum period. I also wasn't doing these concentric contractions in an effort to strengthen or stabilize my body (like I've adamantly urged you to avoid), but with the intention of moving energy.

I share this because if I had just started performing those contractions without having a basis of functional movement first, it would've been equivalent to running without first having the basic mechanics of walking mastered. This is just another way of telling you how important it is for you to do the exercises up to this point in the book before you just try to "fix" your pelvic floor.

I also share it because I've learned so many valuable lessons from the practice of kundalini yoga, including the idea of infodementia. I want you to really understand the concept of a fully functioning body that works as a unit and *works well*, not just the idea that it's a bunch of pieces that are attached.

When you understand that your jaw position impacts how your pelvic floor functions (and I think at this point you do), then you can lean in and trust your body more.

Sometimes all the information that we accumulate from our friends, neighbors, loved ones, doctors, therapists, media, and social media all add up to a massive amount of confusion rather than any tangible help. But if you conceptually understand how the pelvic floor works, then it's easier to recognize what doesn't work to support its function.

When you understand that the core is a pressurized canister, you understand that lifting your couch while sucking in your stomach won't work because that violates the concept of a pressurized canister. When you understand the concept of your pelvic floor moving in response to your diaphragm, ideally you stop holding tension in your abdomen and pelvic floor so the whole system can move and respond normally. When you understand that supporting that pressurized canister means keeping your diaphragm stacked relatively on top of your pelvic floor, you'll rethink that cue that your coach gives you when squatting to keep your chest up, which causes your back to arch.

I want to make sure that this is crystal clear, so here are a few tenets of core and pelvic floor health (which have all been addressed so far in this book) in no particular order:

- keep the diaphragm parallel with pelvic floor for most movements
- avoid dents in the abdominal canister when under load (like sucking in or pulling the pelvic floor up)

- breathe through your nose
- when breathing in, allow your abdomen to expand 360 degrees, but don't force it outward
- when breathing out, allow your abdomen to relax
- relaxation of your abdomen and pelvic floor is as important as contraction
- pressurization - not contraction - creates stability
- sucking in blocks the diaphragm from descending to create pressurization
- expanding your core is not the same as bearing down
- awareness of the pelvic floor is crucial for optimal function
- your daily posture and breathing patterns affect your pelvic floor function
- the health of your tissues will impact your healing time
- scar tissue needs normal sensation and pliability for normal function

An important concept outside of core function that I hope you understand is that your body is self-healing. If you cut your arm, you don't have to tell your blood to clot. It does so on its own. You don't have to instruct your cells to clump together and form a scab or your skin to repair itself with a scar (which you can then mobilize to ensure it moves and feels optimally). These are the benefits of a self-healing body. If you can conceptually understand that your body self-heals, then you can trust your body to heal your pelvic floor from injury, trauma, damage, or poor movement patterns.

This isn't just information that I'm sharing. For many people, this is a paradigm shift.

I'm shifting the onus and the responsibility of helping and healing your own pelvic floor back to you. I'm asking you to take back your own power. Don't rely on external factors to fix your own internal workings. This applies *alongside* the necessity of external care, not exclusive of it. Since your body is self-healing, that means that you are the person who's doing the healing: not your doctor or any external remedy. Yes, those people or tools are working with your body, but it's your body that's actually taking care of business.

And if you are the person who is responsible for your outcomes, then your doctors, therapists, and other practitioners become your guides rather than your dictators. That completely changes the scenario from one where you are a passenger along for the ride to one where you are the driver.

That means that if your doctor gives you a recommendation, you get to consider it rather than take it as gospel. I am not telling you to ignore your doctor's recommendations; I am simply reminding you that you are the person who is responsible for your healthcare. You are a powerful person with the capability of changing your pelvic floor function and you can recruit members to your team to help you along the way.

Exercise - Universe Walks

Trusting your body as a self-healing organism means you need to trust yourself. That's not always easy, especially when your body isn't functioning optimally. I want you to practice trusting yourself, and my friend Sam has an exercise that I think will help.

Samantha Faulhaber is an incredible person and has beautiful intuition and insight that she shares with the world. She gave me permission to share with you what she calls "Universe walks." These walks are your way of tapping into your own intuition. Your intuition is that extra sense that you have when something "feels right" or "feels wrong," and Sam helps people tap into that.

I get that this might be a bit like talking about chakras, but I also want to help you shift your thoughts from one of external dependence to internal trust. If you've read the book *The Gift of Fear* by Gavin DeBecker, you know that the feeling of something being wrong that many people report experiencing before a traumatic event isn't just a random download from the intuition fairy, but all of your observations coalescing into tangible information.[1] This intuitive sense is really the antithesis of infodementia. Your intake of data points at any given moment - things like the air pressure, temperature, smells, patterns, sounds, wind, your own heartbeat, etc. - is so vast that you can't possibly assimilate all of it at every moment, so your brain sifts through what it views as most important. When things go awry, your brain can very quickly tell you to get the heck out of Dodge without your full understanding of why or how you knew to do so.

But it doesn't have to be dramatic or catastrophic. You can tap into your intuition at any time, and the more you do it, the easier it becomes.

I want you to be able to tap into this intuitive sense, and this is a great exercise for doing it. The way Sam explains Universe walks is that you go out for a walk with no predetermined route, but simply follow whatever direction "feels right." Whether you go straight, right, left, backward, or stop is up to how you feel in the particular moment. I think it's fairly obvious that in order to tap into your intuition, you wouldn't be wearing headphones or looking at your phone.

Take these walks as often as you need to (walking is great for reducing your risk of hypertension, hypercholesterolemia, diabetes mellitus, and coronary heart disease) to help tap into your ability to utilize your intuition or recognize your own sense of trust within yourself.[2]

CHAPTER 15

BUILDING A TEAM

I told you at the beginning that this book was not intended for people without a growth mindset. People with a growth mindset realize the endless options that exist and are open to trying new things. People with a fixed mindset already know how things are and are set in their decisions. Because you're reading, I'm assuming that you have a growth mindset, which is legitimately part of actually making improvements. If you believe you are not going to get better, you'll easily create a self-fulfilling prophecy. The same is true if you believe you'll get better.

In the same way, you want your team to comprise people with a growth mindset as well. If your acupuncturist thinks that you shouldn't see the PT, and your PT thinks you shouldn't see the chiropractor, and your chiropractor thinks you should stop consulting with your OB, then your team sucks more than your pelvic floor. To be clear: just because your provider isn't in constant contact or on board with other providers doesn't mean that they suck as individual providers, but they can make your *team* suck.

As a provider, it can be frustrating to work with patients who are getting conflicting information from a variety of providers. And as a provider, I will admit that keeping in touch with other providers is not always an easy task. We generally have protected time at the office where we're seeing patients and can't take phone calls or answer emails. When we're not seeing patients, we need to use that office time to do the other aspects of patient care like chart notes, read labs and images, or investigate treatment options, and in some cases, run our practices. I have time on Wednesdays midday when I will try to set up meetings or phone calls with other providers, but that might not work for their schedule. That means lots of our inter-provider communication is delegated to impersonal faxes or emails or after-hours phone calls that cut into our family/personal time. My point is that keeping communication open between providers can be challenging, especially if our clinical opinions differ.

In my favorite scenarios, I help my patient create their team through established relationships with professionals that I trust and have worked with. This has its limitations because I don't know everyone and because sometimes patients already have several providers on their team by the time they get to my office. But the reason why I like this is because it's really easy to keep open communication with people I know. I work with a great physiatrist (he offers non-surgical pain management like medication and injections) and because he knows what my approach to care is and we've worked together for years, we can just send each other a quick text about referrals.

I do the same thing with the pelvic PTs and other chiropractors I work with regularly.

I'm obviously not sending protected health info via text, but something as simple as: "Sending you a 46-year-old male with right SI pain; crossfitter with clear images but not responding well." He'll know what I mean, and if the case is more complex than that, we can quickly set up a phone call or I'll just give him the head's up that I'll send additional notes over. That's way easier than trying to coordinate a meeting with someone I've never met before who might be a little off-put by the sounds of my rooster crowing and children yelling in the background while I'm at home.

For communicating with providers whose cell phone number I don't have, I use a program called ChiroUp to compile patient reports. With a patient's permission, the same information that they get from me that explains their complaint, what their care will look like, the recommendations I'm giving them, and what exercises they'll be doing is the same thing I share with their provider(s). We don't always have direct communication, but this at least opens the door to what we're focusing on in my office.

Having providers who are willing to communicate with other providers is incredibly helpful when you're dealing with a multifactorial issue like PFD. Teams need leaders and support players and clear, common goals. However, sometimes teams don't sign up as a unit and they just get mashed together in a hodge-podge sort of way. (That probably happens more often than a cohesive team.)

What players ought to be on the team for helping patients with PFD? Well, it depends, of course. The following are providers who help in the care of pelvic floor dysfunction (even if they're not directly *addressing* the dysfunction), in no particular order:

- chiropractor
- pelvic health PT
- orthopedic PT
- acupuncturist
- naturopath
- osteopath
- massage therapist
- midwife
- obstetrician
- gynecologist
- urologist
- urogynecologist
- primary care physician
- physiatrist
- surgeon
- plastic surgeon
- nutritionist/dietician
- counselor/therapist
- dentist
- myofunctional therapist
- coach/trainer

- craniosacral therapist
- shaman or faith-based mentor

I've yet to work with a patient who has all these people on their team, but I've worked with lots of patients who have some much smaller combination of the above list. Hopefully, this far into the book, you can see the value that each of these providers could offer. And keep in mind that if you've tried one of these providers, you haven't tried all of them. Maybe finding the *right* massage therapist will make all the difference for you.

With this many options, that's a lot of potential cooks in the kitchen. Unless all parties are in communication, that's a lot for a patient to juggle. But if we follow a conservative model of care, we will work with the most conservative practitioners and then advance to more invasive practitioners as necessary so that one patient wouldn't actively be under care with the entire list above. At some point, more care isn't better; it's just more.

In addition to players on your team, we can also look at tools. Tools can be things like a journal to help you mitigate stress, or a tangible tool like a pelvic wand (reminder that if you're searching at work, these just look like sex toys). Other tools to consider are things like an infrared or steam sauna, a cold plunge or ice packs, a TENS unit or massage gun. You can also include this book as one of your tools.

Some other potential helpful tools could include things like having a Squatty Potty at all your toilets (your co-workers will appreciate you if you bring one to work) to help ease bowel movements as it allows the pelvic floor to relax into a bowel movement rather than strain while the muscles are attempting to support you in a postural sense.

You could also add in yoni steaming (which is also called v steaming, vaginal steaming, or perineal steaming), wherein you can sit over a pot of herbs in hot water to allow the steam to waft up toward your perineum. This can be a great exercise to combine with journaling or meditation. Before my friend Erika made me a yoni steaming stool, I actually just put a few towels on the base of my Squatty Potty so I could comfortably sit on it and put the steaming herbal water under it. My friend Megan Macpherson is the creator of Yes God Wellness, which is where I get my steaming herbs, and she has a few creative ideas for steaming at home as well that I'll share in the Resources chapter.[1]

I hope that reading this book (and doing the exercises within) will solve your pelvic floor dysfunction. I am guessing you hope that, too. It might. Either way, having caring providers on your team and supportive tools in your tool belt is valuable. Even simply knowing the existence of these providers in your area can be helpful. Perhaps you haven't tried pelvic PT yet, but you ask for a few recommendations from friends or other practitioners already on your team so that if you reach a plateau in your improvement, you'll know who you want to call.

Testimonial

I showed up to Dr. Mumma's office broken, but she was the first one to tell me there was absolutely nothing broken about me.

I was in the postpartum haze being passed between handfuls of providers and offices trying to figure out what was "wrong" with me for months, yet never putting the puzzle pieces together or finding the actual experienced specialists I needed.

And no, a one-time pelvic health course doesn't make you an expert.

Dr. Mumma unlocked the comprehensive treatment plan I needed: chiropractic, manual therapy, women's health education (the one I was never provided elsewhere or growing up), connecting me with a pelvic health PT, and specific rehabilitative exercises customized for my needs following a 40-hour traumatic labor to 9 cm dilation followed by emergent cesarean with extensor cuts on both sides.

Her most effective treatment was listening to me -- validating how I was feeling and searching for my underlying pain. She really was my part-time therapist acknowledging the toll stress and emotions play on recovery.

Under her care I was able to learn what breathing with my diaphragm means (what a concept!), how to down-regulate my nervous system in the most challenging phase of my life, and find the strength to touch, and then massage, my c-section scar.

Dr. Mumma's care did not stop at the end of my first postpartum journey. She helped me prepare for my second pregnancy through micronutrient testing and identifying the correct mix of supplements that I do firmly believe led me to have a regular umbilical cord compared to my nutrient-deficient first pregnancy that had a two-vessel cord.

With ongoing discomfort management, coaching when diagnosed with COVID-19 while pregnant and through a gestational diabetes diagnosis, partnered with my phenomenal midwives, I had a successful vaginal birth after cesarean (VBAC).

My body and mind would not have been ready to welcome my second child had Dr. Mumma not intervened and helped me see the birth trauma I had experienced after my first.

On my second postpartum journey I utilized the same rehab exercises and her "slow is fast" mantra to keep me grounded. We also tackled my vaginal prolapse, which came as a result of having COVID-19 a second time in the early postpartum weeks before my pelvic floor had a chance to strengthen.

While I'm forever grateful to her personally, I'm wildly passionate about advocating for this information to be spread. We need more providers competent in women's health and specifically pelvic health and postpartum care.

- Lauren Hale, 32

Exercise - Things You've Tried

This exercise is for you if you're exhausted from trying multiple ways of improving your pelvic floor with little or no success thus far. If this doesn't apply to you, you can consider this exercise in some other area of your life where you feel frustrated after trying *everything* to make something better.

Grab a pen and paper and make three separate headings: Things I've Tried, Things I Haven't Tried, and Things I Don't Know Yet. One of the frustrations people run into is when dealing in absolutes. If you've tried *everything*, that can feel hopeless because there's nothing left to try. The good news is that it would be truly impossible for you to try *everything*, so it's best to just stick with what's true. This can open up your mind to new (and potentially helpful) experiences or can at least help you identify what might be blocking you from attempting such things.

Until you've tried drinking coconut yogurt through a straw while in a headstand and listening to mantras of pelvic floor empowerment, you haven't tried *everything*. (I am not suggesting you do that. I'm just pointing out that there are lots of possibilities.)

Under the Things I've Tried heading, jot down all of the things you've done in an effort to improve your pelvic floor function (or whatever other challenging situation in your life if you're one of those people reading this whose pelvic floor does not, in fact, suck).

Under Things I haven't Tried, you'll list the things you know about that you haven't yet tried (use the list of providers I shared in this chapter to start). For example, maybe you've tried orthopedic PT, but you haven't tried pelvic PT. Be as specific as possible to help compile an accurate list.

Under Things I Don't Know Yet, leave a big open space because you don't know what you don't know. You'll leave this blank as a placeholder and reminder of your growth mindset: you can always learn new things.

Now, under the Things You've Tried, make a check next to things you've tried to their fullest extent, and circle the things that might be worth re-investigating. If you saw a chiropractor twice when they recommended a treatment plan of four weeks, that would warrant a circle rather than a check mark.

Under Things I Haven't Tried, circle the things you're currently willing to try (as in within the next month, you plan to actively try that option or contact someone to get the process started). Star the things you don't circle that you're not currently willing to try.

From here, set a plan for visiting or revisiting those items you circled. Next, compile the reasons behind the stars you marked. For many people, the reasons for not trying certain therapies are either access or finances. If it's access, meaning that the treatment you would like to try is not in your location, then start to write out what it would take to get you to a location where that specific treatment *is* offered.

If it's finances, make a budget for how much money you need and start a plan for how you can achieve it. I'm not enough of a jerk to tell you how to budget your life, but oftentimes having a plan for how to reach a goal is an impactful step toward reaching that goal. It also makes an *impossible* goal (that's another word that's part of that absolutes category) achievable. It might still be distant, but it's no longer impossible.

Whenever you're feeling incredibly frustrated at your lack of progress, revisit the list, gaze upon the barrenness of the blank space of endless possibilities you don't yet know about, and make a plan toward what an achievable goal for helpful treatment might be.

CHAPTER 16

BRINGING IT ALL TOGETHER

You've got lots of digestible information (some of it was nutritional - see what I did there?), your team, and a growth mindset. Let's do this.

This is the part of the book you've been waiting for, right? You just want to know the one thing that's going to make your pelvic floor stop sucking. I'm with you. But by this point in the book, you hopefully have come to realize that if there was one thing, you'd probably already know it and this would be super simple. The reason why so many people have pelvic floors that suck is because the only thing we've taught them to do is suck. I mean that literally and figuratively. We've only focused on sucking the pelvic floor up and in, lifting your sex organs up to your eyeballs.

That clearly hasn't worked, as we've already discussed. But it's not just because that one thing of kegeling hasn't worked; it's because the pelvic floor is part of a system, and the whole system needs to function better.

The first step is to triage. Obviously, your pelvic floor is a problem because you're still reading. We need to start somewhere to address that, but it might not actually be at your pelvic floor. Another quote from Dr. Lewit is: "He who treats the site of pain is lost," meaning the part of the body making the most noise might not be the cause of dysfunction, just the alarm bell.

In an emergency situation, triage helps to get to the most important matter the most quickly. That's crucial in life-threatening situations. Since your pelvic floor sucking is a matter of quality of life rather than life-or-death, we have a little less pressure on us, but I still want to get this right. Since you're not my patient in this scenario, I can't do the picking for you, which means you're going to need to be honest with yourself (I hope you always are).

I'm going to ask you to characterize your dysfunctions from most to least. I'm not talking about most painful, but most dysfunctional. Thus far we've addressed your breathing, jaw, feet, posture, tension, and nutrition. I have yet to meet a person who is experiencing pelvic floor dysfunction as their *only* dysfunction, even if it is the only symptom they're experiencing. We've talked about it so many times, but the pelvic floor is part of an entire system and isolating it hasn't worked and doesn't help. If it did, I wouldn't have written this book because I wouldn't have *needed* to write this book.

Are you still chest and mouth breathing despite all of my best efforts to the contrary? Does your jaw click every time you open your mouth or chew? Are you rocking bunions on both feet and wearing narrow-toed shoes all day every day (even inside)? Do you know that your posture is terrible and since you started reading this book find that your bowling ball is almost never atop your body? Was the hardest exercise in the book when you had to relax your abdomen and you're covered in trigger points? Did you try to skip the chapter on nutrition because you live on drive-thru meals and Twinkies?

If you answered yes to any of those questions (I really hope you didn't), then you'll need to pick that most glaring dysfunction as the place to begin your focus. Granted, we've already begun some aspects of rehab by the exercises you've done thus far, but I want you to remain focused for at least three weeks on the most glaring issue. That means that if your jaw takes the cake, then you focus on the jaw posture and TMJ exercise (outlined in Chapter 3) for the next three weeks. Maybe you also visit your chiropractor, holistic dentist, or myofunctional therapist. But you at least spend some energy improving your jaw function by performing those exercises twice daily. Continue to do the rest of the exercises in the book, but make your TMJ your main focus for the next three weeks. That will be number one on your list.

I want you to rank any of your dysfunctions as they relate to breathing, jaw, feet, posture, tension, and nutrition. There are six items on that list. Put them in order from worst to least bad, and then address each one for at least three weeks. (If you're doing the math, you have at least eighteen weeks of work ahead of you.) If you're noticing improvements but still have some gains to make (maybe your jaw stops hurting, but you still have some lingering clicking), three weeks isn't a magic end point. It's just a suggestion. Keep working at the things that are not working well so that you can improve them.

It is part of my job as a chiropractor to find the most dysfunctional area of the body to address and create a treatment plan of how to improve function of that area. It is hard to recognize your own faults - and not just in a self-preserving, fixed mindset sort of way. If you're having a hard time, ask someone you trust (whom you don't mind being mad at for a bit when they point out what dysfunction they see), or video yourself doing a set of activities to see what you can pick up from reviewing the footage. This is likely to be more effective than looking in a mirror because you'll be able to see more angles and perspectives of yourself in a video than in a mirror.

I can't guarantee that your pelvic floor symptoms will improve three weeks into working on your most dysfunctional aspect, but for many of my patients, they actually do. In the meantime, your whole body will become more functional, which can lead to your symptoms resolving. Remember: your body knows how to heal. You've seen two of the testimonials in the book reference the mantra of "slow is fast" that I often remind my patients. (That is another gem from Mel Hemphill.) The slower they take their recovery, the faster they'll end up healing. If they try to rush back into activities that they're not fully ready for because their body still needs time to adapt and heal, they'll prolong their overall healing time. This mantra also applies to implementing changes in your lifestyle, eating meals, enjoying the present moment, and more. My friend Claudia says that "slow is fast" applies to everything but traffic.

For the record, you won't get rid of bunion formation in three weeks by any means, but you can significantly improve the direction that your toes point with exercises, devices like Correct Toes, and by changing your footwear to something that allows your feet to splay and move freely.

I want to make a quick note that people think of their feet like they think about scars: not much and not enough. If you don't have obvious bunions or foot pain, you might think you don't need to focus on them. But let's do a quick assessment of your feet to see if they could use some work.

Let's check out your toe strength, for example (we'll call this a bonus exercise since it's not the one I'm putting at the end of the chapter). Start with your bare feet flat on the ground and lift your toes up. Can you easily do ten reps of this without fatigue? Can you tap just your big toes on the ground while the rest of your toes remain elevated? (Can you do it without doing weird movements with your hands? People always get their hands involved when they try to move their toes.) Now can you elevate your big toe and the rest of your toes but keep your pinky toes on the ground?

If you couldn't accomplish these tasks, then your feet do need attention, even if they don't bother you. You can advance your dexterity from here, but that's a great place to start. If your feet are hyperpronated (flat), notice how much you create an arch when lifting your toes up off the ground. Practicing your toe dexterity can help improve your arch strength as well as your ability to feel and respond to the ground.

The three week focus can be helpful for establishing better function in any of the six areas on your own or with help. I'd love it if someone came into my office and said, "Doc, I'd really like to improve my body for the next month. What've ya got?" I've only had a few patients who present like this, but we have so much fun helping their body function better. One patient just wanted better hip and ankle mobility and jokingly said that if I could help him to be able to do a pistol squat (that's a one legged squat where your butt goes at least below your knee), he'd know we were successful. Within two months, he showed me a video of him doing a pistol on the beach. He clarified that the sand might've helped him, but reaching goals like that - which aren't related to pain - can be very helpful when you're slowly and intentionally working toward improvement.

In terms of treatment, I regularly start off with seeing patients twice per week for three weeks so that we can begin with establishing breathing patterns and gradually address whichever dysfunction(s) they show up with. At each visit, the patient demonstrates their exercises and if they're doing them correctly twice daily, I will introduce a new exercise. If they haven't yet mastered the exercise or aren't performing it regularly, I won't introduce anything new. I palpate the joints in their spine and extremities, check for trigger points at each visit, and adjust and do soft tissue work as necessary. I gradually introduce new information regarding overall health as well during this initial phase of care.

After that initial three weeks of care, I typically taper off to once per week for two weeks to make sure that the patient is still showing improvement (from an objective standpoint, not just a subjective one). If they are, we'll skip a week, and if they're still showing improvement after two weeks of not seeing me, then I'll ask them to come back in a month. If they come back and have continued to maintain the functional gains that they previously had attained while under more regular care, I'll recommend they follow up in another month or six weeks to check in and ensure things stay on track.

I don't like to release patients from care until their function has improved, not just when they feel better. There are many dysfunctions that don't hurt a bit. Some patients prefer to continue following up with me because they feel better after getting adjusted and receiving care; some prefer to peace out after their symptoms resolve. In my ideal world, after patients have undergone an initial course of care, they have plenty of tools to take care of themselves for many issues, but will come in for a tune-up every so often to ensure things are moving and functioning well from an objective perspective.

There's a lot that you can do for taking care of your own body, but you can't adjust your own joints in the same way that a chiropractor can.

We can also give hands-on cues to help you understand feedback differently. It's hard to scratch your own back; it's even harder if you don't know where to start itching. For this reason, I don't give pelvic floor lifting or concentric contraction recommendations to patients to perform at home, with the exception of the finger-sucking exercise you did.

I will occasionally add in some pelvic floor lifting movements with patients in my office, but only with hands-on cueing (I'm only doing external cueing and not internal work). It's not something I recommend you practice unless and until someone who knows what they're doing can give you feedback on whether or not you're doing it adequately. Unfortunately, it's not something you can just read about. The exercise you read about earlier (seated breathing with perineum palpation) focuses on the descent, not on lifting the pelvic floor. I find more benefit in patients feeling their pelvic floor descend when palpating their own tissues (or with me palpating them in my office) when they're seated. That exercise is my go-to for troubleshooting pelvic floor dysfunction and is the one I re-introduce immediately if symptoms relapse.

I teach continuing education classes for chiropractors and chiropractic students, and they often ask for a protocol to follow for treatment of PFD. If there was a protocol, I would never have written this book. There are certainly commonalities that show up with patients, but just because the psoas (hip flexor) muscles tend to be tight in lots of patients struggling with PFD doesn't mean that I'm always going to do soft tissue work on the psoas. If there's no tension in your psoas muscles when you come into my office, I'm not going to release them just because that's what is usually required.

I need to match the treatment to the patient, as any good practitioner needs to. You're doing that as well by triaging the dysfunctions you're experiencing in your body. In general, one of the initial triage determinations I make is whether a patient needs more stability or more mobility. This is easier to determine by palpating how their joints move, but can also be determined simply by observing general range of motion. If you can bend forward and put your hands flat on the floor in front of you, you don't need more mobility within your lumbar spine. That doesn't necessarily mean that you need more stability because maybe you worked really hard to get a lot more flexibility, but you do not need more motion. If you can't quite reach your knees when you try to bend forward and touch your toes, you are more likely to need mobility.

Patients who need mobility will require more adjustments and mobility exercises whereas patients who need more stability will require less adjustments and more stabilization exercises. Once I have this basic piece of information determined, I have a better idea of what the patient's care will look like.

A patient who needs overall more stability can very easily feel the need to stretch, and that might make them feel better in the short term, but won't help them overall the way that improving stabilization will. Patients who need more stability almost always feel tight. Their tendency to create muscular tension as a result of the inherent feeling of instability means that their muscles feel tight even though they're lengthened. Those patients might have nagging aches and pains that are setting off alarm bells that the patient often wants to address, but we can often effectively kill two birds with one stone (or feed two birds with one crumb if you're feeling more generous than aggressive) by focusing more attention on the most dysfunctional dysfunction of needing stability rather than trying to calm down all of the alarm bells at one time.

If you've done an honest assessment of your dysfunctions and you spend three weeks focusing on improving each of the six components (breathing, jaw, feet, posture, tension, and nutrition) that are significantly impacting your pelvic floor, you'll likely find yourself with a better functioning pelvic floor in six months. Actually, pull out your calendar and set yourself a little reminder to check in on how your pelvic floor is doing six months from today's date. That way, if you've fallen off the wagon and haven't really been doing any of these exercises, it'll be a nice kick in the pants. And if you haven't fallen off the wagon, you can rejoice in your progress thus far. If you've still got PFD six months from now, but it's improved, then I'd say you're successful and keep at it. While I can't guarantee that you'll have results, I'm pretty confident that addressing these issues will lead to improvements in your PFD symptoms and improvements in your overall health.

Exercise - *Shin Box*

There is something that *most* people can do that will help improve their pelvic function and core stability, regardless of what all dysfunctions they're dealing with: improve their ability to utilize their gluteus (butt) muscles. The glutes sort of drive the pelvis around. When they work well, they can improve posture and pelvic floor function, but most of the time we just smash them under us while sitting all day, which decreases the blood flow and utility of these powerhouse muscles.

We've discussed how improving hip stabilization can help prevent the formation of bunions. Hip stabilization largely refers to the function of the glute muscles. We've already addressed the glutes a bit with hip hinging and the bear position exercise, but I want to introduce you to one of my favorite exercises: the shin box. It's best to do this on a carpeted floor, a yoga mat, or a blanket to keep your bony knees from getting bruised.

The simple way to describe this exercise is to begin with one leg folded in front and the other behind you. But if you're not looking at the videos that accompany this book (check the Resources at the end of Chapter 18), then you might be a little confused. We'll start with the left leg in front and right leg behind. Both knees are bent with your right inner thigh on the floor and your right foot behind you. Bend your left knee and let your leg fall out so that your left inner thigh is now facing the ceiling and your left foot is in front of your body. Your left foot should be contacting (or close to) your right knee. The position has your shins making a right angle to form two sides of a box.

That admittedly sounds really complicated, and if we all spoke the same anatomical language, I could just tell you to flex your right knee, internally rotate your right femur, and place the medial aspect of your right leg on the ground. Then externally rotate your left femur and place the lateral aspect of your left leg on the ground. But what's even easier is if you are familiar with cheerleading jumps: you'll get into a double-hook position on the ground.

If you can sit in this position comfortably with both ischial tuberosities (butt bones) on the floor and an upright torso, then you can move forward. If you can't, place a yoga block, pillow, or blanket (or multiple of each) underneath your left buttock to boost yourself up a bit higher until you are able to sit in this position comfortably and with your shoulders level.

Lean forward slightly without bending at the waist (use your hands on your pubic symphysis and your sternum if you need to!), and press the outside of your front (left) knee into the ground in order to lift your butt off the ground. Avoid using momentum to bring yourself up. Control the movement on the way up to a wide kneeling position (with full hip extension), and then slowly lower back to the ground.

If you aren't feeling this exercise in your butt muscles, then you're most likely using momentum to get out of the bottom position or falling back to your starting position instead of controlling your descent. Start with five reps on each side and build up to ten on each side. Repeat this exercise twice per week.

PART 5

TIMELINES & RESOURCES

CHAPTER 17

TIMELINES

The first time I took a DNS Women's Health course with Martina Ježková, she introduced a concept that was so simple and simultaneously mind-blowing to me. Children potty train around the same time that they jump because upright walking and full integration of the pelvic floor is a necessary component of pelvic sphincter control.[1] It was something I'd never considered at all but made so much sense.

That takes about two-three years to go from absolutely no pelvic control to full jumping capacity. Granted, there are a ton of other factors at play here in terms of upright development and cognitive capabilities, but if we just look at the purely structural aspect, we can go from zero load on the pelvic floor to explosive loading of the pelvic floor in three years, so I think that's at least informative for considering treatment times. It might not take as long for you to go from a dysfunctional pelvic floor to a functional one, but it's possible that it will.

We're the only bipedal (on two legs) mammals whose pelvic floor is entirely underneath our torso and supporting its full weight. Other mammals have a slight forward tilt to their torso that offsets some of the direct downward load onto the pelvic floor. As such, it takes a lot of coordination to create this stability and if it's not working appropriately, it can take a decent amount of re-coordination to establish functional loading.

Perhaps you've heard the old saying that a bumblebee shouldn't be able to fly, but because he doesn't know this, he just does it anyway. It's not true, per se, as bumblebees just create a different vortex of air that helps suspend them compared to other creatures of flight.[2] I tell patients that it's similar for women in the postpartum time period: they can't adequately stabilize like the rest of the bipedal creatures immediately after giving birth, but they figure out another way to do it.

I don't have evidence for this other than my own personal experience and the experience of patient care, but immediately after having a baby, standing and walking feel completely different internally. I noticed this more after the birth of my first son, who was born while I was lying on my side at a birth center. I got up a few hours later to transfer rooms, and I remember distinctly that the idea that I could walk felt foreign to my body. I have spoken to many women who have had a similar experience.

Most of these women birthed in a setting outside of a hospital (home or birth center - or in their car on the way to the hospital). In many hospital births, women aren't walking around as much. Women are a fall risk if they've had an epidural, so they get wheeled around after giving birth. But at some point postpartum, we have to walk, and it feels different. Because tissues are sore and the perineum is often swollen, walking can feel different anyway, but the women I've spoken to all reported feeling like they didn't know *how* to stand or walk. They felt the change in their sensation, not just in their tissues.

If you've not experienced this, I'm sure it sounds weird. If you have, you'll understand why it's really important to consider when we're healing the pelvic floor in the postpartum time period, we have to take into account the unlearning of whatever way we learned to ambulate immediately postpartum. We essentially need to teach a bumblebee to fly like a beetle. It's a totally different pattern.

In most women, they create external (as in the muscles *on* the outside of their own body, not outside *of* their body) stability rather than using their intrinsic (inner) stabilization system because the intrinsic stability has been stretched to capacity and doesn't feel stable. Remember when we talked about creating pressurization and how IAP needed something to resist it? I think this shift from being able to use IAP *with* resistance to *not* with resistance is what my patients and I have experienced immediately after giving birth.

During pregnancy, there's an increase in IAP because there's a human living within the abdominal cavity. This tiny human occupies real estate which disperses IAP, but because it's a closed system, the IAP can't go anywhere and therefore increases. Immediately after the baby is born, that increase in IAP drops drastically. One study (which had some flaws, but provided a measurement nonetheless), showed that prior to birth, median IAP was about 22 mmHg, and dropped to a median of 16 mmHg post-birth.[3] For reference, another study showed us that normal IAP levels in normal-weight individuals vary from sub-atmospheric values to 7 mmHg, and that morbidly obese patients have higher levels: about 9 to 14 mmHg.[4] (All of the studies that I came across admitted that our knowledge of how these pressures truly change during pregnancy is not well known.)

This rapid shifting in pressure levels can be interocepted (felt internally) the next time that stability is required. And for most postpartum women: they don't actually have the stability to stand upright. The combination of the rapid change in how the body stabilizes plus the effects of the process of birth, which is quite arduous, means that the brain needs to figure out a way to accomplish what previously was a relatively mindless task. (The closest non-birth example to this that I've experienced is after a true one rep max lift: the one where you give several high-fives and a few whoops of cheer, but then you're not sure where the ground is because surely there's no possible way you can stand and walk on it after just having completed that endeavor.)

In the early postpartum time period, if a woman then feels the need to not look pregnant any longer, or to squeeze into her old clothes, or start to do more than care for her own body and the life she's just brought into the world, then those early postpartum stabilizing strategies that were meant to be short-lived get the opportunity to persist. She can also encourage these faulty patterns if she starts inappropriately relying on external supportive devices in the postpartum time period.

Belly Binders

For a long time I discounted the idea of binding the abdomen in the postpartum time period because so many women want to do it for aesthetic purposes only. It can be a little disheartening to a woman that after giving birth, she typically looks like she's about six months pregnant. Her abdominal tissues have been stretched to near capacity and that stretched-out feeling isn't just an external view but an internal feeling. There's a hollowness that she often feels post-birth that's likely both physical and energetic in nature.

There was a person who lived inside her body who no longer occupies that space, and it's often a jarring shift from individual to mother-baby dyad for many first-time moms. Because of this, many women experience a very strong desire to gain a semblance of normalcy that their newly-transformed life and body are craving, and cinching down their waist seems an easy (and seemingly harmless) way to achieve this goal.

But while it may be fairly easy for some women to return the core to its former shape using external compression strategies like binders, these are not harmless to a core that needs to fully function.

When I was in college, I played volleyball for a semester at a school where the uniform included ankle braces. I fought with the head coach and trainers about wearing the stupid things because I could tell that they slowed me down. I'd had an ankle injury toward the end of my Junior year of high school season, and had to wear a brace for the rest of the season. I worked really hard to get normal function of my ankle back so that I wasn't dependent upon the brace, and was incredibly dismayed that I would be back in the restrictive devices without an injury that warranted it.

The idea was that they were combating the potentiality of future injury by having athletes wear ankle braces that prevented range of motion of the ankles "within reason." I disagreed and refused to wear them. I didn't have the science to back up my refusal (which I now do and felt quite vindicated when I learned that ankle braces in collegiate volleyball players decreased vertical jump height), but I could tell that the braces weren't doing me any favors.[5] At the time, it just made sense that my own ankles could help me stabilize best.

I applied the same logic of the unnecessary ankle braces to the unnecessary postpartum belly binders for years in my practice.

But the more I studied birthing traditions that had been passed down for centuries from generation to generation in communities and cultures where learning by experience trumps learning by authoritarian dictate, I found benefits to postpartum wrapping.

Notice: I prefer the term wrapping to binding. Wrapping suggests a delicacy and flexibility that binding does not, though these are my word choices and some ancient practices that are truly not restrictive and are indeed flexible and delicate are referred to as "binding." Restricting the movement of the diaphragm in the postpartum time period will serve no mother in her recovery. If you prevent the abdomen from expanding, the pelvic floor will by necessity have to take the brunt of the force being exerted on it.

Some of the benefits included offering warmth to the mother's abdomen. From a Traditional Chinese Medicine standpoint, the prenatal time period is a warm time period and the postpartum period is cold. This is consistent with the rise in the hormone progesterone during pregnancy that increases a woman's basal body temperature, and then drops after the baby is born, leaving a woman with a lower body temp. Many Eastern traditions support this need by serving warm - and even spicy - foods to a postpartum woman.

Bengkung binding is a Malaysian tradition and was recommended to help a woman's organs relocate to their previous positions after giving birth. The expansion of the uterus with a growing baby inside of it causes the woman's organs to move out of the way and into different locations. Wrapping the belly in the postpartum period was intended to help the organs find their way to their appropriate positions.

Another benefit was simply the gift of the time and attention that original wrapping would take. Of course, most Western traditions have modernized the practice - taking what was previously an intricate weaving and braiding of fabric in a slow, contemplative, and meditative practice performed by someone (likely a family member or close friend) who was present to help a woman transition into her role as mother and recover from being pregnant and giving birth into a Velcro strap that can be popped on and off by a woman on her own.

I loved what I was finding, but was a little bit confused with what to do with the information about this beautiful practice because it seemed a little too risky to start recommending that patients begin wrapping their abdomen in the postpartum time period. I was afraid of confusing my patients because I was a little confused how this external support fit into my model of creating internal support within our body.

It all came together when Martina Ježková demonstrated a technique of wrapping a rebozo (a long piece of cloth used to help support a birthing woman) around the abdomen in a DNS Women's Health course. Offering some amount of proprioceptive (body awareness) input into her system by allowing her brain to perceive what her abdomen can (and previously did) feel like when supported can be helpful.

I don't outright recommend postpartum wrapping (as you can tell by the long dialogue I've created around it), but I will sometimes perform a gentle rebozo wrap for a woman while she is in my office. My initial postpartum visits are intentionally scheduled for longer time slots than typical follow-up visits, and this allows me more time to talk with a woman and allow her to share her birth story if she chooses. It also allows me lots of time to re-introduce breathing and posture in the early postpartum days because so much has changed, and to sometimes wrap her abdomen to give her the feeling of stability she may be missing post-birth.

If a woman is using postpartum belly binding for support so that she can run to the grocery store within the first week of giving birth, this can make un-learning those early postpartum pseudo-stabilizing patterns more of a challenge because the faulty patterns have gotten more repetitions. The same is true if she returns to activity (meaning not just workouts, but also daily chores like cleaning or carrying loads of laundry) before adequately recovering postpartum. I recognize that lying in with a baby is a necessary luxury, but a luxury nonetheless. Not everyone who gives birth is surrounded by a supportive partner and community who will carry her through the first days, weeks, and months after having a baby: giving her the grace and space to take her time healing.

Healing takes time (and it's imperative to allow appropriate healing time), but time doesn't heal all wounds. Lots of people assume that if they just give something time, it'll get better. While that's true for flesh wounds, that's rarely the case for dysfunctional movement. If you don't re-pattern a dysfunctional pattern, then it will persist after any amount of rest because that's the easiest pattern for the brain to follow. Your brain is magnificent, but it also takes lots of shortcuts because it's processing so much information that it has to utilize the easy way quite frequently in order to avoid overwhelm.

Since we need to improve not just movement, but tissue health, awareness, and patterns in the brain as well, it is hard to know exactly how long that will take each patient. But as providers, we have expectations for how long it will take for a patient to notice functional changes. A treatment timeline is something that providers talk about in terms of common recovery times or number of treatments. Some professional organizations create what are called "Best Practices" which outline what the - you guessed it - consensus of best practices are.

Expert opinion isn't well-backed by evidence - even when there is a consensus between experts. While saying that, it's still an option for considering what treatment times can be expected. Lots of professions, conditions, and treatment types have Best Practices. I'm currently part of a board that helps write them for chiropractors in North and South Carolina. It's fun to investigate what research says as well as work with colleagues to help guide the "best" practices for our profession.

In terms of pelvic floor function, we've discussed the variety of ways to approach care. General consensus on how long it might take isn't an exact science. All of the factors that play into overall health go into my thought process when determining how long it might take a patient to regain function or recover from an injury. If you've had long-standing PFD without injury, meaning that your symptoms are as a result of multiple dysfunctions adding up over time, then recovery depends on unlearning those dysfunctions as well as training new functional patterns. That will take a totally variable amount of time.

For this reason, it's actually a little bit easier to estimate a treatment timeline for women in the postpartum time period. The way that she gave birth affects her recovery, as well as her overall health during pregnancy and what her postpartum support looks like. It gives us a solid start from essentially a blank slate.

Example Recovery Timeline

If a woman is well-supported immediately after giving birth, she will have the necessary rest to adequately recover before creating repetitions of faulty movement patterns. If a postpartum woman spends the first two weeks co-regulating with her baby and staying fairly sedentary, her tissues can have a better opportunity to heal. Lochia (postpartum bleeding) can be a great checkpoint for women in the postpartum time period because this indicates that there's still healing occurring internally, which often makes it easier to wrap her head around the idea that she still needs to heal even if she starts feeling fairly normal.

The time between two-six weeks postpartum is ideal for recovery. In the same way that after a knee surgery or ankle sprain, you'd spend a few weeks doing gentle range of motion and minimal extraneous activity, a woman in the first six weeks after birth needs to recover as well. Around six weeks postpartum is when most women get a "green light" for activity, but this actually starts the rehabilitation time period: this is when core and pelvic floor rehab can begin. Between four-eight weeks is when I tell my patients to start my Postpartum Rehab program, which is six weeks long. I encourage them to follow that program to a "T" because it lays a solid foundation for continued strength building. If there's no foundation, then a structure will crumble. Her foundation will be a functioning pelvic floor and core. And if she follows the program twice weekly for six weeks, that will bring her to around three months postpartum, which, for many women, is when they return to work (which for most professions means lots of sitting).

I expect most postpartum women to be fully continent by three months postpartum, but recognize that doesn't mean that she's fully healed. If those first three months were spent as described here, she is still not done healing, but she's well on her way to fully recovering. If she returns to work and starts sitting in crappy posture all day, I actually expect that her pelvic floor function will diminish as a result.

From the completion of the Postpartum Rehab program around three months postpartum through twelve months postpartum, I encourage women to focus on rebuilding strength. Any relapses in dysfunction or symptomatic issues (not just in her pelvic floor, but throughout her body) require attention because she's still actively recovering from birth during that time.

Ideally, her recovery doesn't actually stop at one year postpartum; the second year postpartum is great for continuing to replenish nutrients and build strength. That means focusing on form while increasing strength rather than undertaking new challenges. That looks like gradually increasing the weight of her deadlift, taking lifts she knows she can make rather than trying to set a new PR. Or building enough strength to do thirty single-leg squats to a box on each leg before she even considers running. It doesn't mean she *can't* PR her deadlift or return to running: it means she's done that *after* building the adequate strength to achieve those goals.

It also means she prioritizes her meals to be nutrient-dense rather than focusing on how many calories they have, while obviously consuming an anti-inflammatory diet as well as the other components of nutrition we talked about in Chapter 13. She makes visits to her chiropractor and PT a regular occurrence so that her body is moving well.

That's a two year recovery plan for a woman after birth. It sounds like a lot, but that allows her body to adequately recover from the endeavor of creating and birthing a child, as well as replenishing nutrients that were depleted during pregnancy and nursing. That's not even as long as it takes most toddlers to establish the pelvic floor function required for jumping!

Variables in Recovery

For those of you who aren't postpartum, determining a healing timeline can be a little bit more challenging because we're doing that thing where we're teaching bumblebees to fly like beetles: we've got to address all of the reasons why your pelvic floor is communicating with you the way it is, as well as re-learn how to appropriately move. We also aren't starting with a blank slate like we are in the postpartum time period.

You have at least eighteen weeks of rehabilitative work from the previous chapter, so that's a starting point in terms of a timeline, but it's also based on your only spending three weeks on each dysfunction, which might actually require significantly more time to fully address.

Let's put you somewhere between an almost-jumping toddler and a recovering postpartum woman: are you aware of some control of your pelvic floor but are still wetting yourself multiple times per day? You've definitely got more than eighteen weeks of work to do, but that doesn't mean that you won't start seeing improvements right away when you begin implementing more functional patterns and addressing some of the dysfunctions within your body.

As core stability improves, patients tend to notice a variety of changes, but some of the most common are things like less hamstring tension or the ability to hold an upright neutral posture for longer periods of time. Many patients tell me at their initial visit that they think they need to stretch more, but as we improve their breathing mechanics and core stability, they tend to feel more limber without putting any effort into stretching.

As a provider, I'll look for signs of improvement like less trigger points and less joint restrictions. Sometimes a patient's function is improving even though their symptoms are not yet. Sometimes it's easier for the brain to rely on past patterns, even if they're painful, because it's easier than establishing an entirely new way of accomplishing something it already knows how to do. We're asking your brain to have a growth mindset, which isn't always easy.

There's also the possibility that as your function improves, you might actually have an increase in symptoms, specifically stress incontinence. If the pelvic floor has too much tension, and we decrease the tension within it, you might actually leak urine because we just took away your somewhat effective crutch that was holding you up, so to speak. If that is the case, that's not automatically evidence that what you're doing isn't working, but it could cause some rebound tension because the immediate reaction to your pelvic floor leaking urine would be to tighten it right up. For patients who have this response, internal pelvic work (either from a provider or via your hand or a pelvic wand) can be helpful for re-releasing tension and it can also be helpful to wear a pantyliner of some sort. The fear of leaking can cause more pelvic floor tension, and if you have a pad of some sort on, the leaking is less problematic for your wardrobe.

Impact of Intervention

In terms of lasting improvement, some research has shown us that intervention has long-lasting impacts. The PREVPROL (PREVention of Pelvic Organ PRolapse) trial was an RCT performed to determine the impacts of pelvic floor physiotherapy vs. a leaflet. For up to two years post-intervention, the participants with grade one-three prolapse showed continued benefit if they had physiotherapy combined with an at-home exercise program rather than if they just got an informational pamphlet. The participants who had treatment also required less future treatment for prolapse compared to those without treatment.[6]

There is also an argument for early intervention even if you are continent, as a 2020 Cochrane Review pointed out: structured pelvic floor muscle training in early pregnancy may prevent the onset of urinary incontinence later in pregnancy as well as in the postpartum time period.[7] So if you're one of those magical creatures who picked up this book, has a functioning pelvic floor, and is pregnant or plans to be soon, there is a case to be made for pre-emptive intervention to help offset long-term issues.

If everyone started to pay attention to their pelvic floor before they had issues, we'd probably eliminate a significant number of PFD cases. My hope is that when you're done reading this book, you give a well-loved copy to a friend of yours (although I'm not opposed to your purchasing additional copies as holiday and birthday presents for years to come).

Exercise - Child's Pose to DNS Six Month

Child's pose is a common yoga pose, and one that I love for downregulation in general as well as for pelvic floor relaxation. I like to combine this with a DNS exercise that mimics a six-month-old baby on all fours who's rocking back and forth but not yet crawling. It's one of my favorite movements to take the pelvic floor from unloaded and relaxed to activated and working synergistically with the abdominal wall. What I'm saying is this is a great exercise and I hope that I explain it well enough so that you can perform it regularly.

If you're familiar with child's pose (we did it after you released internal trigger points in your pelvic floor in Chapter 6), then start in child's pose and skip the next paragraph.

If you're not familiar with child's pose, then begin on all fours with your knees slightly wider than your feet and your toes pointed and resting on the floor. Walk your hands forward about six inches on each side and then slowly push your hips back toward your heels and continue walking your hands forward until your forehead is resting on the floor, your arms are resting overhead flat on the ground, and your butt is resting on your heels. If you are pregnant, widen your knees so that your belly can rest comfortably between your thighs. If you are unable to get this much flexion in your hips or your knees, use pillows, towels, or blankets to bolster yourself so that you can rest fully in this position (or as close as you can get to it).

Once you are resting in child's pose, breathe fully into your entire abdomen, focusing especially on breathing into your back and into your pelvic floor. In this position, your pelvic floor is being stretched and therefore ideally has no tension in it. Rest here for at least ten full nasal breaths. This is a downregulatory posture for your nervous system as well as an intentional relaxation for your pelvic floor.

In order to come out of the posture and create activation of your pelvic floor, press your hands into the ground to make firm contact with all ten fingers and the big knuckles (your metacarpophalangeal joints if you know which ones those are) and your palms on the floor with your elbows straight.

Begin to shift yourself forward as you press firmly into your hands so that your forearms come off the floor and your pelvis rises off your feet. Pause here and focus on your pelvic floor. Ideally, you'll use your finely tuned interoception and will be able to feel your pelvic floor activating as you hover here. Continue forward movement until you come to a full quadruped (hands and knees) position, but you'll notice that your hands are still at least six inches in front of your shoulders.

Shift your weight further forward while keeping your same pelvic position: do not tip your pelvis forward or backward: keep it centrated. Do this until your hips are fully extended (straightened), which should happen around the same time that your shoulders land squarely over top of your hands. In this position, you ought to feel a lot of abdominal wall activation. Take a breath or two here and slowly return to hands and knees.

If you feel so compelled and really like the feeling of that activation, you can repeat a few reps of the second part of this exercise: begin on hands and knees with hands on the floor in front of shoulders and hips pushed back to the point just before your pelvis tilts toward your feet. Take a breath, feel your pelvic floor activate as you begin shifting forward, and then continue until your hips are extended again and your shoulders are over your hands. Do 5-10 reps. Repeat this at least once per week.

CHAPTER 18

THE REAL END

You made it. We made it. You've reached the conclusion of this book and I hope that you're empowered with more applicable knowledge. I also truly hope that you've implemented the tools in these pages. I don't believe that I have all of the answers. I do think I've outlined a lot of the high points and a lot of these points have helped a lot of people. Unfortunately, the testimonials I have included in this book are all from my patients who have been willing to share their stories. It's not exactly fair to you if you're not a patient because I've put my eyes and hands on those patients and putting *that* into written format for you to self-guide isn't the same. I'm not seeing nor palpating you. I have no idea what your tissues are like.

I do know that the tools included in this book have all been applied to my patients. I also hear from other practitioners whom I've taught in seminars how these tools work for their patients. I don't know how applying these tools outside of patient care will work. I think they'll work well (hence the whole book publication thing), but I can't say for sure.

The patients I've cared for also included the exercises and suggestions of this book - at least some of them - into the care of their pelvic floor, meaning that a lot of their care came not in the form of hands-on manual therapy and chiropractic care.

I want to reiterate that reading this book isn't going to fix or heal your pelvic floor. But *you* can. And you can implement what you've learned here (or you can just read it and move on and not benefit at all from having spent your time reading rather than gardening or creating art or meditating or learning how to speak French - it's up to you).

I am grateful that you've included me in your health journey - whether preventive, informative, or supportive - and hope that you've enjoyed reading this book as much as I've enjoyed writing it. I do have several resources that you are welcome to download to support your journey. These include supplement recommendations, videos of the exercises described in each chapter, a guide on how frequently to implement each exercise as directed, and a one-page summation of this entire book so that you can keep the highlights handy in your brain for those really interesting dinner party topics of conversation.

I hope that you're well on your way to your pelvic floor not sucking.

RESOURCES

Download all of your support handouts at
http://www.yourpelvicfloorsucks.com.

ACKNOWLEDGEMENTS

I would firstly like to acknowledge my very patient husband, Chris. He's the greatest person I've ever met and he truly makes me be a better human. I'm positively mad about him and am eternally grateful for his support as I wrote this book and throughout the entirety of our relationship. I wish I could share him with you but I definitely don't want to.

I also want to acknowledge my sons, Eldon and Calder. They are the most patient children I've ever encountered and I admire their gentlemanly ways. I'm grateful for how much they take after their father and for how forgiving they are of the time that I share with others through my practice, teaching, and writing. I am extremely proud to be their mother.

To those who shared your testimonials in this book: thank you for bravely sharing your vulnerable stories with an unknown audience. I truly appreciate your contribution and hope that someone was able to connect directly with your story as they read this book.

I want to thank my staff at the world's greatest practice, TriangleCRC, for cheering me on: always, but especially as grief took me away from completing this project and I needed some help returning to it. Each of you has played a role in the formation of this book in some way, though I think it's fitting that Mary is the only one that I happened to mention by name in its pages. Mackenzie, Mariel, Peggy, Rebekah, Ashlynne, Caroline, Ashley, and Lisa: you are all amazing individuals and I'm so grateful to have you all on my team. Peggy, you specifically echoed my wantingness to write this book after Vegas, and supported me with writing tools to boot! I'm so glad we all had that incredible trip together (sorry you missed it, Ashley!).

Thank you to my mentors and teachers (many of whom are mentioned in this book), who've helped guide me as a practitioner. I love learning and I'm incredibly grateful to have so many wonderful instructors.

I want to thank my patients for allowing me to learn on a daily basis. Thank you for trusting me with your care. And thank you also for being open to my trying new things and letting me continue to practice and hone my techniques. I will keep learning to better support you.

I want to thank Leah Condon for her incredible help with the citations of this book. I'm not sure how I would've completed the task on my own, and I'm so glad for an opportunity to work with you and for the love you shared while completing it during such a challenging time.

To my editor and potentially long-lost sister, Dr. MaryAnne Dimak, thank you for editing the words here and giving me the grace to extend my deadlines. Your subject matter knowledge and love of the Oxford comma were important aspects of this working relationship, and I'm so honored you said yes to undertaking this project.

Thank you to my coach, Scott Allan, thank you for helping me stay on track and for your guidance throughout the writing process.

To my parents, who are no doubt embarrassed that their daughter wrote a book with "Sucks" in the title even if they're proud of the contents and the accomplishment: thank you for always encouraging my eager brain and supporting nearly all of my endeavors. I'm forever grateful to have been born into our family.

And finally, to you, my dear reader: thank you once again for reading, though I doubt any of you are *still* reading at this point. I'm grateful you put eyes on my words.

CITATIONS

Intro

1 Growth Mindset Book, Dweck, CS. Mindset: The New Psychology of Success. Random House Publishing Group; 2007.

Chapter 2

1 PF as respiration/stability, Hodges, P., Sapsford, R. and Pengel, L. (2007), Postural and respiratory functions of the pelvic floor muscles. Neurourol. Urodyn., 26: 362-371. https://doi.org/10.1002/nau.20232

2 PF strengthening = diaphragm strengthening, Hwang UJ, Lee MS, Jung SH, Ahn SH, Kwon OY. Effect of pelvic floor electrical stimulation on diaphragm excursion and rib cage movement during tidal and forceful breathing and coughing in women with stress urinary incontinence: A randomized controlled trial. Medicine (Baltimore). 2021 Jan 8;100(1):e24158. doi: 10.1097/MD.0000000000024158. PMID: 33429797; PMCID: PMC7793445.

3 Organ movement, Lens E, Gurney-Champion OJ, Tekelenburg DR, van Kesteren Z, Parkes MJ, van Tienhoven G, Nederveen AJ, van der Horst A, Bel A. Abdominal organ motion during inhalation and exhalation breath-holds: pancreatic motion at different lung volumes compared. Radiother Oncol. 2016 Nov;121(2):268-275. doi: 10.1016/j.radonc.2016.09.012. Epub 2016 Oct 20. PMID: 27773445.

4 Breath Book, Nestor J. Breath: The New Science of a Lost Art. Penguin Life; 2021.

5 Stress is good for you, Jacome Burbano MS, Gilson E. The Power of Stress: The Telo-Hormesis Hypothesis. Cells. 2021 May 11;10(5):1156. doi: 10.3390/cells10051156. PMID: 34064566; PMCID: PMC8151059.

6 Civilized to Death Book, Ryan C. Civilized to Death: The Price of Progress. Avid Reader Press / Simon & Schuster; 2020

7 Polyvagal Theory, Porges, S. Polyvagal Th eory: A bi obehavioral Jo urney to Sociality. Compr Psychoneuroendocrinol. 2021; 7. https://doi.org/10.1016/j.cpnec.2021.100069

Chapter 3

1 Creep, hysteresis, and set, Bogduk N. Clinical Anatomy of the Lumbar Spine and Sacrum. Elsevier Health Sciences; 2005:78.

2 Upper Cross Syndrome, Izraelski J. Assessment and Treatment of Muscle Imbalance: The Janda Approach. J Can Chiropr Assoc. 2012 Jun;56(2):158. PMCID: PMC3364069.

Chapter 4

1 Women don't tell their doctors about incontinence, Preidt R. Poll: Women Don't Talk to Docs About Incontinence. WebMD. Published November 1, 2018. Accessed October 21, 2022. https://www.webmd.com/urinary-incontinence-oab/news/20181101/poll-women-dont-talk-to-docs-about-incontinence

Chapter 6

1 Chiropractors applying ischemic compression over the bladder improved UI, Hains G, Hains F, Descarreaux M, Bussières A. Urinary incontinence in women treated by ischemic compression over the bladder area: a pilot study. J Chiropr Med. 2007 Dec;6(4):132-40. doi: 10.1016/j.jcme.2007.10.001. PMID: 19674707; PMCID: PMC2647099.

2 Ischemic compression, Ischemic Compression. Science Direct. Accessed October 21, 2022. https://www.sciencedirect.com/topics/medicine-and-dentistry/ischemic-compression

Chapter 7

1 POP table, Persu C, Chapple CR, Cauni V, Gutue S, Geavlete P. Pelvic Organ Prolapse Quantification System (POP-Q) - a new era in pelvic prolapse staging. J Med Life. 2011 Jan-Mar;4(1):75-81. Epub 2011 Feb 25. PMID: 21505577; PMCID: PMC3056425.

2 MCL healing times, Hildebrand KA, Frank CB. Scar formation and ligament healing. Can J Surg. 1998 Dec;41(6):425-9. PMID: 9854530; PMCID: PMC3949797.

3 Postpartum Rehab course, Postpartum Rehab Course. Triangle CRC. Accessed October 21, 2022. https://www.trianglecrc.com/postpartum-rehab

4 Bunion inheritance, Piqué-Vidal C, Solé M, Antich, J. Hallux Valgus Inheritance: Pedigree Research in 350 Patients With Bunion Deformity. Foot Ankle Surg (N Y). 2007; 46(3): 149-154. https://doi.org/10.1053/j.jfas.2006.10.011

5 Wolff's Law, Jan-Hung Chen, Chao Liu, Lidan You, Craig A. Simmons. Boning up on Wolff's Law: Mechanical regulation of the cells that make and maintain bone. Journal of Biomechanics. 2010; 43(1): 108-118. https://doi.org/10.1016/j.jbiomech.2009.09.016

6 Hip stability and pronation/bunions, Golchini A, Rahnama N, Lotfi-Foroushani M. Effect of Systematic Corrective Exercises on the Static and Dynamic Balance of Patients with Pronation Distortion Syndrome: A Randomized Controlled Clinical Trial Study. Int J Prev Med. 2021 Oct 19;12:129. doi: 10.4103/ijpvm.IJPVM_303_19. PMID: 34912505; PMCID: PMC8631118.

7 Connection of the foot and the pelvic floor, Ježková M. Dynamic Neuromuscular Stabilization (DNS): Women's Health. PDF lecture notes. April 16-17, 2018. Updated: May 13-15, 2022.

8 Barefoot & FiveFingers had greater balance than shoes, Smith BS, Burton B, Johnson D, Kendrick S, Meyer E, Yuan W. Effects of wearing athletic shoes, five-toed shoes, and standing barefoot on balance performance in young adults. Int J Sports Phys Ther. 2015 Feb;10(1):69-74. PMID: 25709865; PMCID: PMC4325290.

9 Bear position increased abdominal wall tension, Madle K, Svoboda P, Stribrny M, Novak J, Kolar P, Busch A, Kobesova A, Bitnar P. Abdominal wall tension increases using Dynamic Neuromuscular Stabilization principles in different postural positions. Musculoskelet Sci Pract. 2022 Aug 14;62:102655. doi: 10.1016/j.msksp.2022.102655. Epub ahead of print. PMID: 35998419.

Chapter 8

1 Dietary collagen supports soft tissue, Bolke L, Schlippe G, Gerß J, Voss W. A Collagen Supplement Improves Skin Hydration, Elasticity, Roughness, and Density: Results of a Randomized, Placebo-Controlled, Blind Study. Nutrients. 2019; 11(10):2494. https://doi.org/10.3390/nu11102494

2 Formation of scar tissue, Martin P, Nunan R. Cellular and molecular mechanisms of repair in acute and chronic wound healing. Br J Dermatol. 2015 Aug;173(2):370-8. doi: 10.1111/bjd.13954. Epub 2015 Jul 14. PMID: 26175283; PMCID: PMC4671308.

3 Vibration can relax muscles and improve circulation, Lee G, Cho Y, Beom J, Chun C, Kim CH, Oh BM. Evaluating the differential electrophysiological effects of the focal vibrator on the tendon and muscle belly in healthy people. Ann Rehabil Med. 2014 Aug;38(4):494-505. doi: 10.5535/arm.2014.38.4.494. Epub 2014 Aug 28. PMID: 25229028; PMCID: PMC4163589.

Chapter 9

1 Basic Childbirth Education Course, Childbirth Education. Triangle CRC. Accessed October 21, 2022. https://www.trianglecrc.com/childbirth-education

2 Fear-Tension-Pain Cycle, Grantly Dick-Read. Britannica. Accessed October 21, 2022. https://www.britannica.com/biography/Grantly-Dick-Read

3 Cryotherapy effects on postpartum perineal pain, Knight K. Cryotherapy Theory: Technique and Physiology. Chattanooga, TN, Chattanooga Corporation. 1985. Accessed October 21, 2022. http://www.cet-cryotherapy.com/cryotherapy_physiologic_effect.html

4 Cryotherapy effects, Knight K. Cryotherapy Theory: Technique and Physiology. Chattanooga, TN, Chattanooga Corporation. 1985. Accessed October 21, 2022. http://www.cet-cryotherapy.com/cryotherapy_physiologic_effect.html

5 Feelings Wheel by Dr. Gloria Wilcox, Kelley, D. Modeling Emotions in a Computational System - Emotional Modeling in the Independent Core Observer Model Cognitive Architecture. Published

2016. Accessed October 21, 2022. https://www.researchgate.net/figure/C-Dr-Gloria-Willcoxs-Feelings-Wheel-9_fig1_303445396

6 What happens in a chiropractic adjustment, Kawchuk GN, Fryer J, Jaremko JL, Zeng H, Rowe L, Thompson R (2015) Real-Time Visualization of Joint Cavitation. PLoS ONE 10(4): e0119470. https://doi.org/10.1371/journal.pone.0119470

7 Adjustments improve proprioception, Haavik H, Murphy B. Subclinical neck pain and the effects of cervical manipulation on elbow joint position sense. J Manipulative Physiol Ther. 2011 Feb;34(2):88-97. doi: 10.1016/j.jmpt.2010.12.009. PMID: 21334540.

8 Adjustments decrease cerebellar inhibition, Daligadu J, Haavik H, Yielder PC, Baarbe J, Murphy B. Alterations in cortical and cerebellar motor processing in subclinical neck pain patients following spinal manipulation. J Manipulative Physiol Ther. 2013 Oct;36(8):527-37. doi: 10.1016/j.jmpt.2013.08.003. Epub 2013 Sep 12. PMID: 24035521.

9 Adjusting a pregnant woman relaxes her pelvic floor, Haavik H, Murphy BA, Kruger J. Effect of Spinal Manipulation on Pelvic Floor Functional Changes in Pregnant and Nonpregnant Women: A Preliminary Study. J Manipulative Physiol Ther. 2016 Jun;39(5):339-347. doi: 10.1016/j.jmpt.2016.04.004. Epub 2016 May 6. PMID: 27157677.

10 Women who receive chiropractic care have shorter labor times, Borggren CL. Pregnancy and chiropractic: a narrative review of the literature. J Chiropr Med. 2007 Jun;6(2):70-4. doi: 10.1016/j.jcme.2007.04.004. PMID: 19674697; PMCID: PMC2647084.

11 Decreased incontinence after adjustment, Zhang J, Haselden P, Tepe R. A case series of reduced urinary incontinence in elderly patients following chiropractic manipulation. J Chiropr Med. 2006 Autumn;5(3):88-91. doi: 10.1016/S0899-3467(07)60139-6. PMID: 19674678; PMCID: PMC2647065.

12 "Laura Palmer" Song, Bastille. Laura Palmer. Published 2013. Accessed November 14, 2022. https://www.youtube.com/watch?v=JQnSc0bczg0

Chapter 10

1 Karel Lewit quotes, Kobesova A. What Has Karel Lewit Taught Us? Prague School of Rehabilitation. Accessed October 17, 2022. https://www.rehabps.com/download/karel_lewit.pdf

2 POP and incontinence, Sublett CM. Pelvic floor muscle training may improve prolapse stage, muscle function and urinary symptoms compared to no training. Evidence-Based Nursing 2013;16:7-8. http://dx.doi.org/10.1136/eb-2012-100798

3 Conservative management of POP, Hagen S, Stark D. Conservative prevention and management of pelvic organ prolapse in women. Cochrane Database of Systematic Reviews 2011, Issue 12. Art. No.: CD003882. DOI: 10.1002/14651858.CD003882.pub4

4 Pessaries and side effects, Bugge C, Adams EJ, Gopinath D, Stewart F, Dembinsky M, Sobiesuo P, Kearney R. Pessaries (mechanical devices) for managing pelvic organ prolapse in women. Cochrane Database Syst Rev. 2020 Nov 18;11(11):CD004010. DOI: 10.1002/14651858.CD004010.pub4. PMID: 33207004; PMCID: PMC8094172.

5 PF muscle training > hypopressive, Resende APM, Bernardes BT, Stüpp L, Oliveira E, Castro RA, Girão MJBC, Sartori MGF. Pelvic floor muscle training is better than hypopressive exercises in pelvic organ prolapse treatment: An assessor-blinded randomized controlled trial. Neurourol Urodyn. 2019 Jan;38(1):171-179. doi: 10.1002/nau.23819. Epub 2018 Oct 12. PMID: 30311680.

6 Estrogen and POP, Ismail SI, Bain C, Hagen S. Oestrogens for treatment or prevention of pelvic organ prolapse in postmenopausal women. Cochrane Database of Systematic Reviews 2010, Issue 9. Art. No.: CD007063. DOI: 10.1002/14651858.CD007063.pub2

7 PF muscle training for dyspareunia, Renata Schvartzman, Luiza Schvartzman, Charles Francisco Ferreira, Janete Vettorazzi, Adriane Bertotto & Maria Celeste Osório Wender (2019) Physical Therapy Intervention for Women With

Dyspareunia: A Randomized Clinical Trial, Journal of Sex & Marital Therapy, 45:5, 378-394, DOI: 10.1080/0092623X.2018.1549631

8 Tampons and toxins, Singh J, Mumford SL, Pollack AZ, Schisterman EF, Weisskopf MG, Navas-Acien A, Kioumourtzoglou MA. Tampon use, environmental chemicals and oxidative stress in the BioCycle study. Environ Health. 2019 Feb 11;18(1):11. doi: 10.1186/s12940-019-0452-z. PMID: 30744632; PMCID: PMC6371574.

9 Catamenial sack patent, Gray AL, inventor. Catamenial Sack. US Patent 626,159. May 30, 1899.

10 About Arnold Kegel, Perry J, Hullett L. The Bastardization of Dr. Kegel's Exercises. Pelvic Toner. Published May 20, 1988. Accessed October 17, 2022. https://www.pelvictoner.co.uk/resources/women-around-the-world-owe-a-huge-debt-to-arnold-kegel.htm

11 PF hypertonicity, Daniëlle A. van Reijn-Baggen, Ingrid J.M. Han-Geurts, Petra J. Voorham-van der Zalm, Rob C.M. Pelger, Caroline H.A.C. Hagenaars-van Miert, Ellen T.M. Laan. Pelvic Floor Physical Therapy for Pelvic Floor Hypertonicity: A Systematic Review of Treatment Efficacy. Sexual Medicine Reviews. Volume 10, Issue 2, 2022. Pages 209-230. ISSN 2050-0521. https://doi.org/10.1016/j.sxmr.2021.03.002

12 SUI and decreased balance, Smith, M.D., Coppieters, M.W. and Hodges, P.W. (2008), Is balance different in women with and without stress urinary incontinence?. Neurourol. Urodyn., 27: 71-78. https://doi.org/10.1002/nau.20476

13 SUI and decreased balance, Smith, M.D., Coppieters, M.W. and Hodges, P.W. (2008), Is balance different in women with and without stress urinary incontinence?. Neurourol. Urodyn., 27: 71-78. https://doi.org/10.1002/nau.20476

14 PF as respiration/stability, Hodges, P., Sapsford, R. and Pengel, L. (2007), Postural and respiratory functions of the pelvic floor muscles. Neurourol. Urodyn., 26: 362-371. https://doi.org/10.1002/nau.20232

15 Low back pain, incontinence, breathing, and GI symptoms, Smith, Michelle D. PhD*; Russell, Anne MMedStat†; Hodges, Paul W. PhD*. The Relationship Between Incontinence, Breathing Disorders, Gastrointestinal Symptoms, and

Back Pain in Women: A Longitudinal Cohort Study. The Clinical Journal of Pain: February 2014 - Volume 30 - Issue 2 - p 162-167. doi: 10.1097/AJP.0b013e31828b10fe

16 Incontinence increases back pain risk , Smith M, Russell A, Hodges P. Do Incontinence, Breathing Difficulties, and Gastrointestinal Symptoms Increase the Risk of Future Back Pain? J Pain. 2009; 10(8): 876-886. Smith, M.D., Coppieters, M.W. and Hodges, P.W. (2007), Postural response of the pelvic floor and abdominal muscles in women with and without incontinence. Neurourol. Urodyn., 26: 377-385. https://doi.org/10.1002/nau.20336

17 TrA fired first in healthy subjects , Hodges PW, Richardson CA. Altered trunk muscle recruitment in people with low back pain with upper limb movement at different speeds. Arch Phys Med Rehabil. 1999 Sep;80(9):1005-12. doi: 10.1016/s0003-9993(99)90052-7. PMID: 10489000.

18 PF muscles delayed in incontinence , Smith, M.D., Coppieters, M.W. & Hodges, P.W. Postural activity of the pelvic floor muscles is delayed during rapid arm movements in women with stress urinary incontinence. Int Urogynecol J 18, 901–911 (2007). https://doi.org/10.1007/s00192-006-0259-7

19 Increased PF muscle activity in incontinence, Smith, M.D., Coppieters, M.W. and Hodges, P.W. (2007), Postural response of the pelvic floor and abdominal muscles in women with and without incontinence. Neurourol. Urodyn., 26: 377-385. https://doi.org/10.1002/nau.20336

20 Feed forward TrA not influenced by direction, Hodges, P., Richardson, C. Feedforward contraction of transversus abdominis is not influenced by the direction of arm movement. Exp Brain Res 114, 362–370 (1997). https://doi.org/10.1007/PL00005644

21 Feed forward TrA is directly influenced by direction, Allison GT, Morris SL, Lay B. Feedforward responses of transversus abdominis are directionally specific and act asymmetrically: implications for core stability theories. J Orthop Sports Phys Ther. 2008 May;38(5):228-37. doi: 10.2519/jospt.2008.2703. Epub 2007 Dec 14. PMID: 18448877.

22 TrA is part of a global system, Morris SL, Lay B, Allison GT. Transversus abdominis is part of a global not local muscle synergy during arm movement.

Hum Mov Sci. 2013 Oct;32(5):1176-85. doi: 10.1016/j.humov.2012.12.011. Epub 2013 Mar 5. PMID: 23482302.

23 Corset hypothesis rebuttal, Morris SL, Lay B, Allison GT. Corset hypothesis rebutted--transversus abdominis does not co-contract in unison prior to rapid arm movements. Clin Biomech (Bristol, Avon). 2012 Mar;27(3):249-54. doi: 10.1016/j.clinbiomech.2011.09.007. Epub 2011 Oct 13. PMID: 22000066.

24 IRD increased in suck-in group, Mota P, Pascoal AG, Carita AI, Bø K. The Immediate Effects on In ter-rectus Di stance of Ab dominal Cr unch an d Drawing-in Exercises During Pregnancy and the Postpartum Period. J Orthop Sports Phys Ther. 2015 Oct;45(10):781-8. doi: 10.2519/jospt.2015.5459. Epub 2015 Aug 24. PMID: 26304639.

Chapter 11

1 Exercising Through Your Pregnancy Book , Clapp J. Exercising Through Your Pregnancy. 2nd ed. Addicus Books; 2012.

2 Do not sit your babies, Mumma, L. On Their Own: How to Stop Interfering with Your Child's Development. Pathways to Family Wellness. Published 2019. Accessed October 21, 2022. https://pathwaystofamilywellness.org/childrens-health-wellness/on-their-own-how-to-stop-interfering-with-your-childs-development.html

3 Altered PF muscle activation, Thompson JA, O'Sullivan PB, Briffa NK, Neumann P. Altered muscle activation patterns in symptomatic women during pelvic floor muscle contraction and V alsalva manouevre. Neurourol Urodyn. 2006;25(3):268-276. doi: 10.1002/nau.20183. PMID: 16496395.

4 Previous writings about diastasis, Books by Lindsay Mumma. Amazon. Accessed November 14, 2022. https://www.amazon.com/Lindsay-Mumma/e/B01L49V25M/ref=aufs_dp_fta_dsk

5 Previous writings about diastasis, Diastasis Rectus Abdominus. Triangle CRC. Accessed October 21, 2022. https://www.trianglecrc.com/articles/diastasis-rectus-abdominis

6 Prevalance of diastasis, Sperstad JB, Tennfjord MK, Hilde G, Ellström-Engh M, Bø K. Diastasis recti abdominis during pregnancy and 12 months after

childbirth: prevalence, risk factors and report of lumbopelvic pain. Br J Sports Med. 2016 Sep;50(17):1092-6. doi: 10.1136/bjsports-2016-096065. Epub 2016 Jun 20. PMID: 27324871; PMCID: PMC5013086.

7 IRD increased in suck-in group, Mota P, Pascoal AG, Carita AI, Bø K. The I mmediate E ffects on In ter-rectus Di stance of Ab dominal Cr unch an d Drawing-in Exercises During Pregnancy and the Postpartum Period. J Orthop Sports Phys Ther. 2015 Oct;45(10):781-8. doi: 10.2519/jospt.2015.5459. Epub 2015 Aug 24. PMID: 26304639.

8 Mini crunch load on lumbar spine, Stuart M McGill, Low Back Exercises: Evidence for Improving Exercise Regimens, Physical Therapy, Volume 78, Issue 7, 1 July 1998, Pages 754–765, https://doi.org/10.1093/ptj/78.7.754

9 Pre-activation of TrA stops IRD from decreasing, Lee D, Hodges PW. Behavior of the Linea Alba During a Curl-up Task in Diastasis Rectus Abdominis: An Observational Study. J Orthop Sports Phys Ther. 2016 Jul;46(7):580-9. doi: 10.2519/jospt.2016.6536. PMID: 27363572.

10 Combo of both types of abdominal muscles would be best, Michalska A, Rokita W, Wolder D, Pogorzelska J, Kaczmarczyk K. Diastasis recti abdominis - a review of treatment methods. Ginekol Pol. 2018;89(2):97-101. doi: 10.5603/GP.a2018.0016. PMID: 29512814.

Chapter 12

1 Lifetime risk of POP or SUI surgery, Wilkins MF, Wu JM. Lifetime risk of surgery for stress urinary incontinence or pelvic organ prolapse. Minerva Ginecol. 2017 Apr;69(2):171-177. doi: 10.23736/S0026-4784.16.04011-9. Epub 2016 Dec 21. PMID: 28001022.

2 Chiropractic care or orthopedic surgery, Keeney BJ, Fulton-Kehoe D, Turner JA, Wickizer TM, Chan KC, Franklin GM. Early predictors of lumbar spine surgery after occupational back injury: results from a prospective study of workers in Washington State. Spine (Phila Pa 1976). 2013 May 15;38(11):953-64. doi: 10.1097/BRS.0b013e3182814ed5. PMID: 23238486; PMCID: PMC4258106.

3 PRP injections, Platelet Rich Plasma (PRP) Injections. Hopkins Medicine. Accessed October 24, 2022. https://www.hopkinsmedicine.org/health/treatment-tests-and-therapies/plateletrich-plasma-prp-treatment

4 PRP for PFD, Prodromidou A, Zacharakis D, Athanasiou S, Protopapas A, Michala L, Kathopoulis N, Grigoriadis T. The Emerging Role on the Use of Platelet-Rich Plasma Products in the Management of Urogynaecological Disorders. Surg Innov. 2022 Feb;29(1):80-87. doi: 10.1177/15533506211014848. Epub 2021 Apr 28. PMID: 33909538.

5 Manipulation vs. surgery for LBP, McMorland G, Suter E, Casha S, du Plessis SJ, Hurlbert RJ. Manipulation or microdiskectomy for sciatica? A prospective randomized clinical study. J Manipulative Physiol Ther. 2010 Oct;33(8):576-84. doi: 10.1016/j.jmpt.2010.08.013. PMID: 21036279.

6 Prostatectomy and incontinence, Haglind E, Carlsson S, Stranne J, Wallerstedt A, Wilderäng U, Thorsteinsdottir T, Lagerkvist M, Damber JE, Bjartell A, Hugosson J, Wiklund P, Steineck G; LAPPRO steering committee. Urinary Incontinence and Erectile Dysfunction After Robotic Versus Open Radical Prostatectomy: A Prospective, Controlled, Nonrandomised Trial. Eur Urol. 2015 Aug;68(2):216-25. doi: 10.1016/j.eururo.2015.02.029. Epub 2015 Mar 12. PMID: 25770484.

7 Native tissue vs. mesh, Maher C, Feiner B, Baessler K, Christmann-Schmid C, Haya N, Marjoribanks J. Transvaginal mesh or grafts compared with native tissue repair for vaginal prolapse. Cochrane Database Syst Rev. 2016 Feb 9;2(2):CD012079. doi: 10.1002/14651858.CD012079. PMID: 26858090; PMCID: PMC6489145.

8 Mesh Recall - FDA News Release., FDA takes action to protect women's health, orders manufacturers of surgical mesh intended for transvaginal repair of pelvic organ prolapse to stop selling all devices. Food and Drug Administration. Published April 16, 2019. Accessed August 21, 2022. https://www.fda.gov/news-events/press-announcements/fda-takes-action-protect-womens-health-orders-manufacturers-surgical-mesh-intended-transvaginal

9 Improved incontinence after POP surgery, Khayyami Y, Elmelund M, Klarskov N. Urinary incontinence before and after pelvic organ prolapse surgery-A national

database study. Int Urogynecol J. 2021 Aug;32(8):2119-2123. doi: 10.1007/s00192-021-04738-6. Epub 2021 Feb 26. PMID: 33635353.

10 QoL improved 2 years post POP surgery, Mattsson NK, Karjalainen PK, Tolppanen AM, Heikkinen AM, Sintonen H, Härkki P, Nieminen K, Jalkanen J. Pelvic organ prolapse surgery and quality of life-a nationwide cohort study. Am J Obstet Gynecol. 2020 Jun;222(6):588.e1-588.e10. doi: 10.1016/j.ajog.2019.11.1285. Epub 2019 Dec 11. PMID: 31836546.

11 Minimal evidence for pre-operative care, Haya N, Feiner B, Baessler K, Christmann-Schmid C, Maher C. Perioperative interventions in pelvic organ prolapse surgery. Cochrane Database Syst Rev. 2018 Aug 19;8(8):CD013105. doi: 10.1002/14651858.CD013105. PMID: 30121957; PMCID: PMC6513581.

12 Bariatric surgery improved PFD, Lian W, Zheng Y, Huang H, Chen L, Cao B. Effects of bariatric surgery on pelvic floor disorders in obese women: a meta-analysis. Arch Gynecol Obstet. 2017 Aug;296(2):181-189. doi: 10.1007/s00404-017-4415-8. Epub 2017 Jun 22. PMID: 28643025.

13 Adding rehab to sling surgery, Sung VW, Borello-France D, Newman DK, Richter HE, Lukacz ES, Moalli P, Weidner AC, Smith AL, Dunivan G, Ridgeway B, Nguyen JN, Mazloomdoost D, Carper B, Gantz MG; NICHD Pelvic Floor Disorders Network. Effect of Behavioral and Pelvic Floor Muscle Th erapy Combined With Surgery vs Surgery Alone on Incontinence Symptoms Among Women With Mixed Urinary Incontinence: The ESTEEM Randomized Clinical Trial. JAMA. 2019 Sep 17;322(11):1066-1076. doi: 10.1001/jama.2019.12467. PMID: 31529007; PMCID: PMC6749544.

Chapter 13

1 Deflame Diet, Seaman, D. Deflame Enterprise. Accessed October 24, 2022. www.deflame.com

2 Food is Medicine, Hyman M, Bradley E. Food, Medicine, and Function: Food Is Medicine Part 1. Phys Med Rehabil Clin N Am. 2022 Aug;33(3):553-570. doi: 10.1016/j.pmr.2022.04.001. Epub 2022 Jun 25. PMID: 35989051.

3 Collagen peptides for improving recovery, Kviatkovsky SA, Hickner RC, Ormsbee MJ. Collagen peptide supplementation for pain and function: is it

effective? Curr Opin Clin Nutr Metab Care. 2022 Nov 1;25(6):401-406. doi: 10.1097/MCO.0000000000000870. Epub 2022 Aug 31. PMID: 36044324.

4 B12 deficiency and bone fractures, Pawlak R. Vitamin B12 status is a risk factor for bone fractures among vegans. Med Hypotheses. 2021 Aug;153:110625. doi: 10.1016/j.mehy.2021.110625. Epub 2021 Jun 5. PMID: 34116377.

5 Low B12 and depression in pregnancy, Peppard L, Oh KM, Gallo S, Milligan R. Risk of depression in pregnant women with low-normal serum Vitamin B12. Res Nurs Health. 2019 Aug;42(4):264-272. doi: 10.1002/nur.21951. Epub 2019 May 22. PMID: 31119757.

6 Structured water improves health (animal study), Michael I Lindinger, Structured water: effects on animals, Journal of Animal Science, Volume 99, Issue 5, May 2021, skab063, https://doi.org/10.1093/jas/skab063

7 Weston A. Price nutrition info, Weston A. Price, DDS. Weston A. Price Foundation. Published January 1, 2000. Accessed October 24, 2022. https://www.westonaprice.org/health-topics/nutrition-greats/weston-a-price-dds/#gsc.tab=0

8 Postpartum Depletion, Serrallach, O. The Postnatal Depletion Cure: A Complete Guide to Rebuilding Your Health and Reclaiming Your Energy for Mothers of Newborns, Toddlers, and Young Children. Grand Central Publishing; 2018.

9 Postpartum supplements improve vaginal healing, Takacs P, Kozma B, Lampé R, Sipos A, Poka R. Randomized controlled trial for improved recovery of the pelvic floor after vaginal delivery with a specially formulated postpartum supplement. Obstet Gynecol Sci. 2020 May;63(3):305-314. doi: 10.5468/ogs.2020.63.3.305. Epub 2020 Apr 3. PMID: 32489975; PMCID: PMC7231945.

10 Normal vaginal flora, Saraf VS, Sheikh SA, Ahmad A, Gillevet PM, Bokhari H, Javed S. Vaginal microbiome: normalcy vs dysbiosis. Arch Microbiol. 2021 Sep;203(7):3793-3802. doi: 10.1007/s00203-021-02414-3. Epub 2021 Jun 13. PMID: 34120200.

11 L. Rhamnosus for BV, Recine N, Palma E, Domenici L, Giorgini M, Imperiale L, Sassu C, Musella A, Marchetti C, Muzii L, Benedetti Panici P. Restoring vaginal

microbiota: biological control of bacterial vaginosis. A prospective case-control study using Lactobacillus rhamnosus BMX 54 as adjuvant treatment against bacterial vaginosis. Arch Gynecol Obstet. 2016 Jan;293(1):101-107. doi: 10.1007/s00404-015-3810-2. Epub 2015 Jul 5. PMID: 26142892.

12 Lactobacillus for GBS, Liu Y, Huang Y, Cai W, Li D, Zheng W, Xiao Y, Liu Y, Zhao H, Pan S. [Effect of oral Lactobacillusrhamnosus GR-1 and Lactobacillusreuteri RC-14 on vaginal Group B Streptococcus colonization and vaginal microbiome in late pregnancy]. Nan Fang Yi Ke Da Xue Xue Bao. 2020 Dec 30;40(12):1753-1759. Chinese. doi: 10.12122/j.issn.1673-4254.2020.12.09. PMID: 33380389; PMCID: PMC7835693.

13 Vitamin D and PFD , Badalian SS, Rosenbaum PF. Vitamin D and pelvic floor disorders in women: results from the National Health and Nutrition Examination Survey. Obstet Gynecol. 2010 Apr;115(4):795-803. doi: 10.1097/AOG.0b013e3181d34806. PMID: 20308841.

14 Vit D, skin, and eye exposure, Desotelle JA, Wilking MJ, Ahmad N. The circadian control of skin and cutaneous photodamage. Photochem Photobiol. 2012 Sep-Oct;88(5):1037-47. doi: 10.1111/j.1751-1097.2012.01099.x. Epub 2012 Feb 21. PMID: 22277067; PMCID: PMC3371101.

15 Light therapy improves male sexual function, D. Koukouna, L. Bossini, I. Casolaro, C. Caterini, A. Fagiolini, P.4.b.010 - Light therapy as a treatment for sexual dysfunction; focus on testosterone levels, European Neuropsychopharmacology, Volume 26, Supplement 2, 2016, Page S606, ISSN 0924-977X, https://doi.org/10.1016/S0924-977X(16)31685-6

16 Sitting decreases circulation, Hartman YAW, Tillmans LCM, Benschop DL, Hermans ANL, Nijssen KMR, Eijsvogels TMH, Willems PHGM, Tack CJ, Hopman MTE, Claassen JAHR, Thijssen DHJ. Long-Term and Acute Benefits of Reduced Sitting on Vascular Flow and Function. Med Sci Sports Exerc. 2021 Feb 1;53(2):341-350. doi: 10.1249/MSS.0000000000002462. PMID: 32826636.

17 Phthalates disrupt hormones , Palacios-Arreola MI, Morales-Montor J, Cazares-Martinez CJ, Gomez-Arroyo S, Nava-Castro KE. Environmental pollutants: an immunoendocrine perspective on phthalates. Front Biosci (Landmark Ed). 2021 Jan 1;26(3):401-430. doi: 10.2741/4899. PMID: 33049675.

18 Intermittent fasting can improve insulin sensitivity in women, Arbour MW, Stec M, Walker KC, Wika JC. Clinical Implications for Women of a Low-Carbohydrate or Ketogenic Diet With Intermittent Fasting. Nurs Womens Health. 2021 Apr;25(2):139-151. doi: 10.1016/j.nwh.2021.01.009. PMID: 33838849.

19 Women with insulin resistance have less PFM activity , Micussi MT, Freitas RP, Angelo PH, Soares EM, Lemos TM, Maranhão TM. Evaluation of the relationship between the pelvic floor muscles and insulin resistance. Diabetes Metab Syndr Obes. 2015 Aug 28;8:409-13. doi: 10.2147/DMSO.S85816. PMID: 26357485; PMCID: PMC4559236.

20 Shift workers and disrupted sleep negatively impact hormones and fertility , Lateef OM, Akintubosun MO. Sleep and Reproductive Health. J Circadian Rhythms. 2020 Mar 23;18:1. doi: 10.5334/jcr.190. PMID: 32256630; PMCID: PMC7101004.

Chapter 14

1 The Gift of Fear Book , DeBecker G. The Gift of Fear: Survival Signals that Protect Us from Violence. Dell Publishing; 1999.

2 Benefits o f w alking , W illiams P T, Th ompson PD . Wa lking ve rsus ru n-ning for hypertension, cholesterol, and diabetes mellitus risk reduction. Arterioscler Thromb V asc B iol. 2 013 M ay;33(5):1085-91. d oi: 1 0.1161/ ATVBAHA.112.300878. Epub 2013 Apr 4. PMID: 23559628; PMCID: PMC4067492.

Chapter 15

1 Setting up perineal steaming at home, Macpherson M. Options For How to Vaginal Steam At Home - DIY Tutorial. Published Jul 26, 2018. Accessed October 24. 2022. https://www.youtube.com/watch?v=4-ue8syxX2k&

Chapter 17

1 Potty training and jumping happen around the same time , Ježková M. Dynamic Neuromuscular Stabilization (DNS): Women's Health. PDF lecture notes. April 16-17, 2018. Updated: May 13-15, 2022.

2 Bumblebee flight , Thomas A. The Bumblebee Flight Myth. Animal Dynamics. Accessed October 25, 2022. https://www.animal-dynamics.com/the-bumblebee-flight-myth/

3 IAP pre- and post-birth, Chun R, Kirkpatrick AW. Intra-abdominal pressure, intra-abdominal hypertension, and pregnancy: a review. Ann Intensive Care. 2012 Jul 5;2 Suppl 1(Suppl 1):S5. doi: 10.1186/2110-5820-2-S1-S5. Epub 2012 Jul 5. PMID: 22873421; PMCID: PMC3390298.

4 IAP Levels , Staelens AS, Van Cauwelaert S, Tomsin K, Mesens T, Malbrain ML, Gyselaers W. Intra-abdominal pressure measurements in term pregnancy and postpartum: an observational study. PLoS One. 2014 Aug 12;9(8):e104782. doi: 10.1371/journal.pone.0104782. PMID: 25117778; PMCID: PMC4130571.

5 Decrease in jump height with ankle braces , You DZ, Tomlinson M, Borschneck G, Borschneck A, MacDonald M, Deluzio K, Borschneck D. The Effect of Ankle Brace Use on a 3-Step Volleyball Spike Jump Height. Arthrosc Sports Med Rehabil. 2020 Aug 20;2(5):e461-e467. doi: 10.1016/j.asmr.2020.04.015. PMID: 33134981; PMCID: PMC7588605.

6 Evidence Based PF treatment, Gamse C. Evidence-Based Prevention and Treatment of Pelvic Floor Dysfunction. Medpage Today. Published March 24, 2017. Accessed October 25, 2022. https://www.medpagetoday.com/resource-centers/urinary-tract-health/evidence-based-prevention-and-treatment-pelvic-floor-dysfunction/1034

7 Pre- and post-natal PFMT for postpartum UI, Woodley SJ, Lawrenson P, Boyle R, Cody JD, Mørkved S, Kernohan A, Hay-Smith EJC. Pelvic floor muscle training for preventing and treating urinary and faecal incontinence in antenatal and postnatal women. Cochrane Database Syst Rev. 2020 May 6;5(5):CD007471. doi: 10.1002/14651858.CD007471.pub4. PMID: 32378735; PMCID: PMC7203602.

ABOUT THE AUTHOR

Lindsay Mumma, DC, is a practicing chiropractor and the owner of Triangle Chiropractic and Rehabilitation Center in Raleigh, NC, a multidisciplinary practice she opened in 2012 after graduating from Palmer College of Chiropractic with the Clinical Excellence Award. She teaches continuing education for the Motion Palpation Institute and moveMentors. Her private practice focuses on rehabilitative chiropractic care across the lifespan and with a specific focus on prenatal and postpartum health. She is a wife, mother to two boys, speaker, life enthusiast, and author of *The Trimester Series* and the Substack publication *Dr. Lindsay Mumma's Newsletter*.

Made in the USA
Columbia, SC
23 May 2023

16958273R00164